TIS GRACE THUS FAR

THE AMAZING GRACE STORY OF
BOBBY BRITT

Copyright 2011, Bobby Britt

All Rights Reserved

Published by Bobby Britt Evangelistic Association

Printed by Create Space

With sincere appreciation to Teri Smith for the many hours spent preparing the book for print.

TABLE OF CONTENTS

Chapter 1	No Place Like Home	11
Chapter 2	Moving To the New House	23
Chapter 3	Salvation and Sadness	30
Chapter 4	A Boy Beguiled	39
Chapter 5	Choices and Consequences	43
Chapter 6	Mastered by the Master	50
Chapter 7	Craving for the Classroom	53
Chapter 8	College Days	56
Chapter 9	Revival Flames	63
Chapter 10	Memorable Moments (Not too Spiritual)	74
Chapter 11	Off to Seminary	81
Chapter 12	Man Does Not Live by Bread Alone	84
Chapter 13	On Other's Shoulders	89
Chapter 14	He Proves Himself Faithful	93
Chapter 15	Surprise, Another Boy	97
Chapter 16	Back to Alabama	99
Chapter 17	Charting Through New Waters	111
Chapter 18	Plowing New Ground	117
Chapter 19	A Great Dilemma	119
Chapter 20	A Faith Stretching Event	123
Chapter 21	Quartering at The Queen Mother's House	136
Chapter 22	On To Nkawka	143
Chapter 23	Lonely in a Crowd	148
Chapter 24	All Good Things Must Come to an End	159
Chapter 25	The Inner City Ministry	166
Chapter 26	The Dark Valley Ministry	169
Chapter 27	Sufficient Grace	175
Chapter 28	The Unseen Hand of God	178
Chapter 29	Preparing for the Transplant	183
Chapter 30	The Day of Deliverance	187
Chapter 31	Another Open Door	191
Chapter 32	Hypochondriac?	194
Chapter 33	Still Waters Disturbed	198
Chapter 34	Peace in the Midst of the Storm	203
Chapter 35	Whom the Lord Loves He Disciplines	208
Chapter 36	A Different Ministry	212
Chapter 37	Possessing Our Possessions	214
Chapter 38	And in Conclusion	224
Chapter 39	Instruments of God	231

DEDICATION

TO MY WIFE CAROLYN
WHOM GOD HAD IN MIND WHEN HE SAID,
"IT IS NOT GOOD FOR MAN TO DWELL ALONE"

AND

TO OUR THREE SONS
WHO HAVE MADE ME PROUD TO
BE CALLED "DADDY"

PREFACE

At first glance, a title like "TIS GRACE THUS FAR" does not lend itself to be a dynamic, attention grabbing designation for a book. Perhaps it is somewhat innocuous until a person really grasps the depth of meaning of that word, 'Grace'.

The old Baptist definition of 'unmerited favor' is certainly true, but oh, so limited, so inadequate. In II Corinthians, chapter twelve, we find the Apostle Paul crying out to God for the removal of his thorn in the flesh. His is confronted by the refusal of the Father as to the removal, but he is comforted by the promise of 'sufficient Grace'. If the definition of grace is limited to 'unmerited favor' what comfort does this assurance provide in the midst of his tremendous suffering?

In reality, grace is not just an attribute of God, but it is also the *activity* of God. Grace is the supernatural, the Divine *activity* of our living Lord that is available and sufficient for every event in our walk with the Savior.

It is with that understanding I have chosen to entitle this memoir of my story. For reasons known only unto Him, our faithful Lord has chosen to guide me through some deep valleys in this sojourn. Though I have often failed to appropriate that Divine activity from time to time, He has brought me to my spiritual senses and I have found that Grace more than sufficient for every testing and trial. More than a few times I have written with reluctance and a self-consciousness that this volume might appear to be a plea for sympathy or the ramblings of a hypochondriac. If I know my heart, which no one does, the intent of this autobiography is written that He might be glorified, and with the desire that a testimony may be given that it is:

'By Grace Thus Far and Grace Will Lead Me Home!'

FOREWORD

The inevitable problem of speaking about one's self is the insidious danger of unseemly pride. Apart from a strong dose of humility and a God given touch of discernment, very few can escape the trap of inflated opinions of who we are and what we have done. The person who has never been tempted to brag probably hasn't yet been born. Oscar Levant is said to have once asked George Gershwin, "Tell me, George, if you had it to do all over, would you fall in love with yourself again?" Unfortunately, most of us have that depraved disposition to love ourselves.

That unsavory and vain proclivity probably explains Paul's stern warning when he wrote, *"For I say, through the grace given unto me, to every man that is among you, not to think of himself more highly than he ought to think..." (Romans 12:3).*

In this delightful autobiography, Bobby Britt has managed to escape that subtle trap that has so often befallen others. With remarkable grace and wisdom, he has succeeded in telling the readers what God has done for him without unduly boring them with all he has done for God. With a winsome touch of humor and a heavy dose of self-abasement, he has woven together an unusually charming and easy to read synopsis of his greatly blessed life.

Bobby Britt has been my friend for over fifty years – and I count him among my most treasured acquaintances. From the first day we met at Howard College (now Samford University) in Birmingham, Alabama, I knew there was something very special about him. He had an unusual and engaging touch of charm and it was obvious even then that the

Lord was going to use him is some significant way. And indeed He has!

With great joy and thanksgiving, I have watched as he ascended the pinnacles of success – and have often been saddened as I observed him trudging through the valleys of despair. Seldom, if ever, have I met anyone who endured more trials and tribulations. But to his credit, and great praise to God's enabling grace, he has done so with a surprising and commendable absence of whining and complaining.

I am extremely excited that he has now chosen to share his enchanting testimony with others. Every Christian should read this book – but especially those who feel the call to full-time ministry. It is indeed good news for those who find themselves in bad times.

I sincerely pray that the dear Lord shall give this laudable volume a hearty reception and a wide circulation.

Evangelist Junior Hill

Hartselle, Alabama

A LITTLE TASTE OF HONEY

It was late that Sunday night in the fall of 1955 as Mother and I stood in the dining room of our home and opened the white envelope. Tears of gratitude and unbelief brimmed my eyes as I counted the five, brand new, crisp, uncirculated $20.00 bills. The most cash money I had ever held in my hand and it was mine. It represented the first honorarium I had ever received for preaching a revival meeting. What was so overwhelming was not the amount of money, but that I had actually been rewarded for the privilege of experiencing the most fulfilling, enjoyable week of my entire life, eight nights of preaching God's Word and seeing forty-nine people coming to claim Jesus as their Savior and Lord.

Now, more than fifty years later that sense of awe still remains. In my wildest imagination I could have never dreamed of the joy and satisfaction that the succeeding years would bring. I trust that the following pages will accurately describe the thrill of the journey and the gratitude of my heart for His call upon my life.

Surely no one begins such a task without some reluctance. It is inevitable that an autobiography is filled with 'I's and 'Me's which seems to border on the egotistical, but praying that is not the lasting impression of these pages, I begin.

CHAPTER 1

NO PLACE LIKE HOME

It was indeed a good home into which I was born, but it was not a Godly home. Mom and Dad were members of the Sixty-Sixth Street Baptist Church, but we seldom attended as a family. My mother's aged parents lived with us and demanded almost constant care. Granny was beset by dementia and Pappy suffered from a heart condition. More than once Granny would, somehow, get out of the house and wander the neighborhood. With great alarm we would scurry the area, imagining the worst possible scenario, but not once did she come to harm. She would sit for hours in their bedroom and converse with imaginary people of years gone by. It was understandably difficult for Mother to attend church.

Daddy was a tough railroad man with a tendency for alcohol that resulted in tears and turmoil for the family. I can still hear Mother, after my brother and I were in bed, pleading with him to quit drinking. One of the most vivid recollections is that of being awakened in the wee hours of the morning to hear Mother frantically calling friends and neighbors to arrange bond. He had wrecked the 1939 Plymouth and was arrested for DUI. I recall the shame I felt when a police car pulled to the curb in front of the house the next morning and Dad emerging after a night in the Birmingham Jail. More than once he would make a promise to me only to break that pledge because of booze.

Perhaps the one that grieved me the most was when he promised to take me to my first football game, but didn't follow through. It was during grammar or grade school when I was about eight years old. One of my best friends, a doctor's son, was constantly bragging about going to Legion Field to watch the Woodlawn Colonels play. In my envy, I pled with

Dad to take me to a game. Finally, as boys can do, I wore down his resistance and he agreed to carry me on the coming Friday night. Excitedly, I told my buddy and others that I would see them at the game. Friday afternoon I came in early from play and bathed (and it wasn't even Saturday), changed clothes, combed my hair, and anxiously awaited his arrival. Five o'clock, six, six-thirty passed and no anticipated appearance. I was broken hearted and Mother was more than angry. I was mad and miserable. How could I face my friends come Monday morning? I fell asleep on the living room couch and late, late that night I heard the door open and close, and Daddy staggered into the living room, drunk. It was nearly thirty years later that the Lord brought that scene before the eyes of my memory and I knelt by a bed in a motel room and confessed my sin of unforgiveness. It was a moment of liberation for me.

And yet, in spite of all this, he was a loving, caring father and sharing these experiences in no way is meant to dishonor my Dad. Not once was there ever any sort of abuse and never can I recall a curse word from his lips. It is with fond memories that I recall sitting around the radio listening to Gang Busters, The Green Hornet, Inner Sanctum, etc. as we would sit at the card table and put together 1,000 piece jigsaw puzzles or play Chinese Checkers.

Most Monday nights would find us at the 'raslin matches', cheering Tarzan White and Farmer Brown and booing the Bat, the Golden Flash and their kind, as they gouged the eyes and pulled their dirty tricks on my heroes of the ring. The best memories of Daddy were the fishing trips to East Lake Park and Lake Purdy.

His job as a railroad man required him to often be away from home and I can recall the excitement when he returned on Friday afternoons, always with some small gift for Bubba and me.

We certainly were not poor, nor rich; I guess we would fall into that blue-collar category. I recall Mother's delight when Daddy purchased linoleum to cover the bare floor in the kitchen and the pride at having an oilcloth to cover the kitchen table. Not once can I remember Dad getting a vacation nor do I recall any family in the neighborhood taking a week or two to enjoy the beach. It was the post depression years and we lived in a rental house in East Lake. As mentioned, Granny and Pappy had their bedroom, Mom and Dad theirs, and my brother I and shared the same bed. Our room was heated by a small fireplace and on especially cold nights Dad would warm bricks, wrap them in towels, and tuck them at the foot of the bed to warm our feet. Bubba, almost nightly, had vivid nightmares. It was not unusual to hear him scream me awake, sit up in bed, point to the window with eyes wide open and describe the monster coming in the screen. The next night it would be a rat or snake descending from the ceiling. In my half wakened stupor, cold chills would envelop my body, as I believed the wild stories. One night he actually threw his clothes out the window onto the front porch, went outside and dressed, pushed his bicycle down the steps, and rode down the street toward the paper branch to start throwing his papers. Riding down First Avenue North he awakened and headed back home, crawled back into bed and finished his sleep.

We did have a sister, sixteen years older than me, and as the little brother, I was the apple of her eye. She worked for the Telephone Company and before I began grade school she was diagnosed with Tuberculosis. In those days, TB often meant quarantine in a medical facility. Understandably, unwilling to submit to that decision, she left home to live with an aunt in Denver, Colorado where there was less pollution in the Mile High City. I missed her terribly.

THE ALMOST PRODIGAL

It was a really happy childhood with one exception. I cannot remember the cause of the occasion, but it had to be significant, because I decided to run away from home. At five years of age, I had had it. I informed my mother of my displeasure and voiced my intent to vacate the premises, knowing that she would be heartbroken. To my utter amazement she packed me a few clothes in a paper sack and made me a sandwich for my evening meal on the road. She kissed me goodbye and I walked down the back steps expecting to hear her tearful entreaty to please not go. Taking half dozen steps I turned to wave and she returned the same. Reaching the middle of the back yard I turned to say my last goodbye and she bid me her last farewell. Finally, I reached the back fence, covered with honeysuckle, and lifting my leg over the last barrier to freedom, I issued my last goodbye and she just waved. With disgust and disbelief, I did an about face, plodded up the steps and told her that I had decided not to break her heart and would remain at home.

As I look back these many years later I wonder if she wasn't glad to get rid of her little stinker!

CHICKS AND PEG LEG

One memorable day, Daddy brought home a box filled with little yellow chicks. We were going into the chicken and egg business. He built a small hen house and installed a wire fence. It was exciting to watch the little biddies grow into man and womanhood. For some reason, one of the two roosters developed a crooked leg and walked and ran with a distinct limp. His deformity resulted in him becoming a fierce fowl with long sharp spurs. I delighted in gathering the eggs from the small hen house, but to do so, I would have to get down on my all fours to reach the hen's nests. More than a few times, while in my crouched position, old Peg Leg would jump on my back and dig those spurs into my flesh and bring blood. For some fowl reason, that old rooster entertained a special loathing for Reggie Harp. Whenever he would even attempt to enter our back yard, Peg Leg would run full speed ahead and chase him out of the yard and down the alley till he was out of sight. One of the happiest days of that era was when I walked home from school one day and noticed that my mortal enemy was nowhere to be found. When I asked his whereabouts, I was informed that Daddy had wrung his neck and buried him in the ash pile. Peg Leg spurred the wrong member of the Britt family, met his match and paid the supreme sacrifice.

Though we lived in the city, it was permissible for folks to have animals in their yard. My buddy, Ralph Loveless, had two goats in his back yard, but what delighted me most was the cow and barn owned by Mr. and Mrs. Kimble who lived on the corner of 70th Street and First Avenue North. They were strictly country folks and to a little boy of five they seemed ancient, though they were probably in their fifties. Corn on the cob was a special treat for me because it was one of my few favorite vegetables, but of far greater joy, it meant that I could carry the corn shucks to the old dilapidated barn and hand feed their milk cow. Not only did we buy milk from Mrs. Kimble, but also I often watched her churn butter with great fascination and then bring home that fresh golden product.

Just across the street from the Kimble's was the 'Twin Barrels', a raucous honkie tonk, where beer flowed freely and loud jukebox music penetrated the night air. The sinful place of shame was less than a city block from our house, but we were warned to never set foot on the premises. The best way to be sure a kid will try something is to tell him he can't, so often we would sneak down to the little Sodom and peer through the screen widows and watch the Prodigals gyrate to the music.

DAYS OF PATRIOTISM

These were the days World War II era and patriotism was a hallowed quality. We hated the Japs. They had so cowardly attacked Pearl Harbor. I can still remember sitting on the front porch when news of the Sunday morning invasion occurred. I was only five at the time, but realized something serious had taken place.

My patriotism consisted of 'playing army' with my buddies and only the Lord knows how many Germans and Japanese we slaughtered in the neighborhood. None were ever wounded or taken prisoner, all were terminated. We were always victorious, maybe wounded, but we never lost a battle.

Daddy was an Air Raid Warden and I was so proud of him. Fairly often there would be a practice run, a blackout, and all the lights in every home and business and every streetlight would be extinguished. There was the potential threat that the Germans would somehow cross the Atlantic and rain down bombs on the city. It was Daddy's responsibility to put on his armband, take flashlight in hand and go around the entire block to make sure that all lights were out. Of all the dads in the neighborhood, he was the only Warden to my knowledge and he was my hero.

One would have had to live in those days to appreciate the country's loyalty to the military and to the entire war effort. I remember Daddy purchasing a War Bond on two specific occasions. One of those purchases gave the family the privilege of a close up, hands on inspection of a Japanese suicide submarine. Looking through small portholes we viewed two Japanese dummy sailors, manning the sub and the tips of two torpedoes protruding on the front of the vessel. The other purchase gave us an entrance to Legion Field where a full-scale battlefield was simulated. There were mortars firing, rifles and machine guns blazing, canons blasting and the enemy soldiers were falling like flies. Not even a football game elicited the emotion and cheering that could be heard erupting from the stadium that night.

My brother and I did our part by buying 'Victory Stamps' toward the purchase of War Bonds. Stamps were ten and twenty-five cents each and sold every Tuesday. We would proudly purchase those stamps at Barrett School, lick them and stick them in a special book. When you had enough to fill an $18.75 cent book you tucked them away. When the bond matured, some years later, you could redeem the same for $25.00.

It was with eager anticipation that we looked forward to going to the theater and watching the newsreels that gave us an up close look at the war. With interest we listened to the nightly news. Those were the days of rationing and a sticker was placed on the windshields of automobiles to determine what days and how many gallons of gas you could purchase a week. Sugar, coffee and many other goods were rationed and always in short supply. Our military men needed these commodities and little griping was ever heard. Only the most vile neighbors were those who hoarded in their pantries. My complaint was that there few Hershey bars, Mounds, Milky Ways or Three Musketeers available and being a chocoholic since the womb, I did feel deprived.

About the middle years of the war, U.S. Army trucks would pass down First Avenue in front of our house carrying gray-garbed German prisoners on the way to incarceration camps in Anniston, Alabama, just north of Birmingham. I would hiss and hurl insults at the captured soldiers; I felt it was my patriotic duty, but deep down I must confess a sort of pity I felt for them, though I would never admit it.

It was during these days that my sister met an Army Air Force fellow. He was a proud Texan (are there any other kind?) and he was stationed in Denver, Colorado where she had fled to find a cure for the spot on her lungs. They fell in love and were married. He was a side gunner on a B24 and one day his fifty- caliber machine gun exploded, seriously injuring his face and eyes. At first they said he would be blind in one eye, but after some time his vision returned.

We had never met Joe, but I was proud of my new brother in law. A picture of him rested on top of our piano and I would place one finger over his right eye, trying to imagine how he would look with his injuries. One would think such an experience would result in a discharge, but not so when the outcome of the war was still in doubt. He was shipped overseas to England and flew numerous bombing runs over Europe. He told how he was on one particular mission when blazing UFOs were spotted, an event never seen before. These were the first buzz bombs or V2 rockets fired on England from positions in Germany.

GONE BUT NOT FORGOTTEN

There was something special about those days. The war with Japan and Germany brought a cohesiveness to the entire nation. At old Barrett School there seemed to swell a particular pride within the breast of every child when we daily pledged allegiance to Old Glory. We closed those solemn moments with the words, "I thank God that I am an American." Even though we were small children and could not possibly have understood the complexities of a World War, that pledge never seemed routine or said simply out of rote memory. At every ballgame, at the playing of the National Anthem and the Colors were raised, people stood reverently to their feet, with a hand over the heart. To this very day, tears brim my eyes when I hear a recording of Kate Smith sing, 'God Bless America.' I don't know what happened to that patriotism, that sense of loyalty to this great country, but I fear that we have lost something, never to be regained.

MORE MEANDERINGS OF THE MIND

Another fond memory lodged in my boyhood days. We lived on First Avenue North, the main four-lane street in Birmingham. Down the center of the street were two sets of parallel rails. One set of tracks went east and the other set west. The old wooden streetcars or trolleys clattered those rails night and day. At the rear of the motor vehicle was a boom that reached up to electric lines overhead. This was the main method of transportation in the city. Families were fortunate to own an automobile and only the wealthy could afford a second.

We boys took delight in placing pennies on the rail and watched as the iron wheels smashed the coins flat as a flitter. You could then punch a hole at the top and make a pendant. We would also take coke caps that would be popped off the bottles. Inside the cap was a cork seal and we would remove the seal, place as many match heads as possible, replace the seal and take delight in hearing the loud pop when the wheels would crunch the homemade explosive. On a few occasions we came into possession of dangerous railroad torpedoes. These were about 2x2 inch pouches filled with black powder, capsulated in thin metal. Originally intended to alert a railroad engineer of a problem ahead of the engine, they were placed on the tracks to warn him of danger. On the tracks of a streetcar, they would rattle the windows of houses and slightly rock the heavy streetcars.

As I walk down memory lane, I think of the street vendors who would walk down the sidewalks of the neighborhood, hoisting pallets above their heads and calling out, "Strawbeeeeries, strawbeeeeries," at the top of their lungs. I would plead with Mother to please purchase their delicacies. But best of all reminiscences are those of the mustached gypsy organ grinders that would come once or twice a year. One could hopefully hear the music in time to rush out and see the smiling old gentleman with the monkey on his shoulder. I was so fascinated by the frisky little fellow dressed in his bright red jacket with little gold buttons and a tiny bellhop's cap on his head, held secure by a little leather strap under his chin. What a thrill it was to have the petite jungle creature leap to my shoulder and take a coin from my hand to drop in the master's tin cup. I begged mother and daddy to buy me a pet monkey, but the request was denied and they assured me that one monkey in the family was enough.

ALLEY CATS

For some reason, when we went to school or the theater, we seldom walked the sidewalks, but preferred the alleys. It is amazing what boys can stumble on among the discards left beside the garbage cans. Today such items would find their way to garage sales, not existent in those days. We searched for any metal items that might later be a source of revenue. It was a glorious day, indeed, when we happened upon a discarded water heater. The heaters back then were large galvanized tanks, with no insulation, and a gas burner on the bottom. It would require four of us to lug the find to our back yard. With bated breath, we would await the day when the junk man would come down the alley in his mule drawn wagon hollering out, "Scrap iron, scrap iron." With pride we would display our collection and bargain the best price we could negotiate. Pennies, nickels, dimes and quarters were like dollar bills today.

TREASURE FOUND

As already mentioned, we were not poor, but we were certainly not wealthy, and any added income was greeted like a long lost friend. One night we were playing chase or a type of hide and seek. Right next door to our house was a Gulf Service Station. Located behind the building was a large wooden box that was used to store lumps of coal for the little pot bellied stove in the station. The box was about the size of a large chest freeze with a hinged lid. I decided that container would be the perfect hiding place. Raising the top, I crawled into dark abyss and smiled as I heard the searchers run back and forth trying to find 'Little Britt.' As I nestled in the black as midnight hideout, I felt an odd cellophane package. When the seekers finally gave up I raised the lid in triumph, proud of my illusive choice of a chamber. As I made my exit, I asked for help in removing my find in the coal bin. It was with gleeful amazement that we discovered the package contained twelve dozen fudge brownies from the famed Floral Park Bakery. They were probably the fruit of some person's thievery, hidden away temporarily, but now it was 'finder's keepers loser's weepers.' We enjoyed a dozen of the delicacies, but went door to door the next morning, selling our wares at bargain prices. We deemed ourselves young entrepreneurs.

A FATHER'S SHAME

The Lyons lived just across the alley from our house. Most intriguing about the family was the huge apple tree that nestled in their backyard, just a few feet from the alley. In part, I can identify with Eve in the garden when she looked and lusted after the forbidden fruit. One day, Bubba and I and a couple of the guys could stand it no longer. Creeping into the backyard, we shimmied up the tree, filled our pockets with the produce and sat down behind the thick honeysuckle hedge on the edge of our yard. We were enjoying the fruits of our thievery, bragging how we had outwitted 'Old Lady Lyons' when there came that eerie awareness that someone was standing behind us. Turning around, my heart stopped when I saw Daddy staring at his two wayward sons and their friends. I didn't need the whipping, so justly deserved. His obvious shame and disappointment would have been punishment enough.

I have often contemplated how our spiritual lives would be enriched if we could live with constant awareness of our Heavenly Father's presence, our every action under His watchful eye, and the hurt that our conduct brings to His loving heart.

CHAPTER 2

MOVING TO THE NEW HOUSE

Our new brick home. One of only a few pictures with my Dad, Mom, and brother Frank, or Bubba.

It was 1944 and my parents decided it was time to quit paying rent and finally buy a house of our own. Though the new dwelling was only six blocks from the rental abode, it seemed miles away. We were off the noisy First Avenue North, no more clattering streetcars and constant traffic. We were now in a quiet neighborhood where we could skate, ride our bikes and play football and baseball in the street. We would always choose up sides to form the teams. I was often the last one chosen, but I vividly remember one of the first chosen, Nellie Tice. That's right, a female that was feared by almost all the guys. We had observed her, unmercifully, assault and battering Donald M., a guy much larger than me. Even if I could have whipped her, how do you brag about 'whippin' up on a female? Usually in jeans, she was 'Hades on Wheels.' Nobody messed with Nellie. She would pop you with an elbow to the nose in a second and when she threw a pass, it wasn't some little effeminate half throw, it was a bullet. I have often wondered what became of dear ole' Nellie, pity the poor fellow who married her.

As to the new house, we now had a central heating system, a huge coal-burning furnace located in the basement and a cellar that brought its own special intrigue. The only lights down there were the ones above the furnace and one over the large area for storing the large lumps of coal. I was responsible for feeding the fiery monster and removing the burned out clinkers. I did so with a wary eye toward the dark, the ominous area behind the furnace. I envisioned all sorts of monsters and creatures hiding in the shadowy quarters. I don't know why, but I felt there was some protection as long as I whistled during the task.

BLESSED PRIVACY

Most appreciated about the new residence was the fact that I had my own room and my own bed. No more having to call out to Daddy, "He's on my side, he's touching me, make him move over, etc." Best of all, no more bloodcurdling cries in the night as Bubba saw his snakes and rats and monsters creeping through the windows or coming out of the walls. His nightmares persisted into his adult life. He almost received a medical discharge from the Air Force when he got up one night, turned on the lights in the barracks and hollered, "Hit the deck, time to get up!" The bleary eye recruits began to bail out until someone realized it was two a.m. and he had gone back to the sack. They did to him what I had wanted to do all my life.

The new residence came with a small chicken house with nice separate boxes for the hens to lay their eggs. It was with regularity that Daddy would venture into the fenced area, and choose a chicken at random, grasp the poor creature about the head and with few swift revolutions of his wrist, break the neck. With amazement I would observe the doomed bird flip and flop for several minutes after being decapitated. It just did not make sense that a headless fowl could still flutter about. (I later read in Bob Ripley's Believe It Or Not column of a headless chicken that lived for weeks in that condition. He or she was fed and watered though a tube implanted in the neck. Gruesome.)

THE EXECUTIONER

Once, when Dad ventured out the back door to carry out the hen house execution, I requested the privilege of letting me do the 'fowl' deed. He caught the ole' gal and handed her to me and with evil intent I seized her by the neck, gave ten or fifteen twirls for good measure, and released the bird to watch her do the death dance on the ground. To my bewilderment, rather than hitting the turf, she flew into the top of the pear tree and stayed there for two days. Pop laughed at my failure and then explained that to properly accomplish the feat, I had to tightly hold the bird's head and not simply let the neck rotate with the chicken.

I am afraid that few women today can even imagine slaughtering a chicken in the morning, removing the entrails, dropping the carcass in a bowling pot, and pulling all the feathers from the creature, then lighting a rolled up newspaper to burn away the remaining pinfeathers, dismember the body and have it deliciously fried and placed on the table by noon. Ah, the good ole' days! I can promise you that no store bought fowl compares in palatability with the ground scratching, home grown bird of yesteryear.

GOOD OLD DAYS

When someone says things today are not like they were in the 'good ole days', I think of the reply, "They never were." But, my boyhood days were good old days. They were the days when you were fortunate to own an automobile and no family we knew of had two. The old '39 Plymouth was not a luxury car and was not intended to be, it was just a means to get you where you were going. It had four in the floor, hand cranked windows and no heater. It was a treat, on Sunday afternoons, to load up the family and drive around the city, park beside the road at the airport and watch the airplanes take off, drive to see the statue of Vulcan, make our way over the mountain to glimpse at the houses of the 'sure nuff' rich folks, and come back by Pipers Ice Cream Store for a double dip cone. How sedate and boring that must seem to this generation of youth today, but I still contend, God permitted me to come along in the 'good ole' days'.

FAMILY VACATIONS

What was a vacation? My brother and I cannot remember Dad ever taking a vacation nor can I remember any of my buddy's families taking a vacation. Oh, there were occasions when the family would travel to Elmore County, to the little cotton mill town of Tallassee, Alabama, where Daddy was born. He was one of nine boys and two girls, but had run away from home as a teenager when his father remarried and he and his stepmother just couldn't get along. The trip was made about once a year during the Thanksgiving or Christmas holidays and was always an adventure of excitement. Most of the houses were mill village dwellings, all built on the same order and all painted white. It was here that I ate my first breakfast of fried chicken with homemade biscuits and gravy. Most of our relatives were just plain old country folks and proud of it. Dressed in their overalls and brogan shoes, there was absolutely no pretense or put on; my kind of individuals till this very day.

Many recollections stand out about those visits, but two I will mention here. I will never forget my first witness to hog killing time. Venturing out to the smelly hog pen, Uncle Oscar lifted his rifle and shot old porky right between the eyes. She fell with a thud and my young heart pounded and experienced tinges of sadness, but I dared not give expression because my cousins looked on with glee and I didn't want to be the chicken hearted, city slicker. Several adults hoisted old Porky up and hung her dead carcass by her hind legs and I will save you the gory details that followed. Even before the murderous shot had been fired, a large wash pot had been filled with water, which was now in a rolling boil. In a little while, the inner portions of the sow were placed into the liquid and I was later offered my first experience of trying to eat 'chittlins', but to no avail. They tasted horrible and the more I chewed, the larger they became, and with disgust I spewed them out of my mouth to the insulting laughter of my country cousins.

SPITTIN' IMAGE

The other recollection was one of pride. Almost every night all the family would gather in a room around an old fashion fireplace, constructed only to keep the place warm, and not for ornamentation. There would be all the adults, Uncle Oscar and Aunt Luzille and their three boys, my Mom and Dad and Bubba and me. We kids were fascinated as they related the stories of years gone by, work in the mills and whatever came to mind. Aunt Luzille sat in her rocker with a generous wad of Garret Snuff under her lower lip and every few minutes would firmly press the first two fingers of her right hand on her lips, and with a sudden burst of oxygen from her lungs, expectorate (spit) a brown stream of gook, right into the open fire. It landed with a sizzle and puff of smoke and not one drop would hit the floor, though she sat five feet away! Where was the pride of which I spoke? It was the statement she would make during the conversations. She would look at me and then at my Dad and comment, "Bobby, son, you are the *spitten* image of Bill Britt." Daddy was my hero and nothing so thrilled my heart as to be compared with him, though I never understood the stream of snuff analogy.

A SPIRITUAL AWAKENING

Though spiritual things were not a priority in the Britt household, God began to sovereignly move upon my heart with a desire to become a Christian.

On a few occasions my parents would attend The Birmingham Gospel Tabernacle located downtown. It was a large brick building with hard pews and heated by several glowing potbellied stoves. It was during WW II and the dynamic pastor, Dr. Glen Tingley, was a prophecy scholar. There was much speculation about the Anti-Christ, Hitler's attempt to exterminate the Jews in Europe, Mussolini's ruthless dictatorship of Italy and his Roman rule. Surely prophecy was being fulfilled before our eyes and the return of Jesus was on the horizon. My understanding was certainly limited, but I do remember the fear that filled my heart at the thought of being left behind at His coming.

As I look back on those times, I realize I was under conviction and needed a Savior. Knowing of my concern my mother invited the pastor of the Sixty-Sixth Street Baptist

Church to come to our home to share the plan of salvation with me. I can still recall the Saturday morning that Brother Scroggins was to arrive and the mixed emotions of my heart. There was gladness and sadness. A glad prospect about being saved and sadness in that I feared certain failure in answering the Bible questions I was sure to be asked. The moment of destiny arrived and the black Chevrolet pulled to the curbing in front of the house. In a few moments this humble man of God sat next to me with an open New Testament and walked me through the Roman Road. I needed no convincing of my sinfulness, of that I was well aware. Cheating in school, lying myself out of trouble, and a myriad of other things plagued my heart and mind. What really caught me off guard was when he asked me, "Bobby, does God love sinners?" and I quickly responded, "No, sir." I thought, to myself, that is why you go to Hell and surely to earn the favor of God you had to quit sinning. Never will I forget as he turned to Romans 5:8 "But God commendeth his love toward us, in that, while we were yet sinners, Christ died for us." I am so glad I missed the right answer and there on that Saturday morning Jesus graciously heard the prayer of a little boy and took up residence in my heart and life.

When someone questions if a child of nine, not raised in a committed Christian home, having no recollection of an open Bible in his home nor hearing a mother or father audibly pray, can experience genuine conversion, I assuredly affirm, "Yes!" It was just as amazing to know that God began to deal with my heart about preaching His Word by the time I was ten. Some skeptic challenges, "How do you know that?" The only response is, "I just know that I know." And after more than fifty-five years of ministry the reply is just the same.

CHAPTER 3

SALVATION AND SADNESS

Following my public profession of faith in Jesus as Savior and baptism there was a growing awareness that God had put within my heart a desire to preach His Word. I vividly remember writing in a little red dairy that concern. Another recollection of those days was that of the pride that swelled within my heart as I saw my Dad now taking us to church and later being asked to teach a class of young men. A cherished picture that yet lingers in my memory is that of seeing him standing on the sidewalk beside the church building, along with other men, waiting for the worship service to begin. I still joke about the fellows gathering to offer up burnt sacrifices (Lucky Strike and Camels) just before the service.

The arguments between Mother and Daddy now ceased and no longer did he come home drunk. Soon he quit his railroad job and entered the insurance business. I am convinced it was because the Lord had used my salvation to speak to his heart and he was trying to make a break with an environment that offered too many temptations.

Dad's new occupation brought about a door of opportunity to open an office in Shreveport, Louisiana. For a number of months he would come home on some weekends and I can still remember the sorrow and sadness of my heart as I sorely missed him. I thought to myself, "When I become a father I won't stay away from my family like this." Little did I suspect that a few years later God would call me into evangelism making it necessary for me to be away from my wife and children.

Finally, Mother went to be with Daddy in Shreveport in order to purchase a home and upon her return, our house in Birmingham went on the market and our plans were made to move. It was with excitement that I looked forward to a new city and mainly because Daddy had told me how close we would be to the Red River and that meant fishing, the lifelong delight of my life.

Mom and Dad. Taken by a street photographer in Shreveport just days before his sudden death.

Some days later, our home in Birmingham sold and final plans for the family to move to our new home in Louisiana were completed. On a Saturday morning in May of 1946, my brother, Bubba, and I were in the back yard bathing our cocker spaniel, getting him spic and span for the trip. The moving van was to come on Monday and load the furniture and we were to board a train and make our way to Shreveport. Our older sister came to the back porch frantically sobbing words of distress. We rushed up the steps into the house and found Mother screaming out her disbelief as she stood in the hallway with phone in hand. Someone had called to notify her that they had just found Daddy dead in his hotel room, the victim of a massive cerebral hemorrhage. Never will I forget the immediate nausea and pain that I felt in the pit of my stomach as those words, "Daddy's dead," sank into my ten year old heart. In the confusion of the moment I made my way back to my bedroom and falling across the bed crying out to God, "Don't let this be true, let it be someone else's daddy." In the midst of my deep grief, God brought back to my mind the messages I had heard in that Birmingham Gospel Tabernacle about the soon return of the Lord Jesus and God graciously blessed my heart with the assurance of seeing my Dad again when He comes. To this day, that truth is the message I delight to preach above all others. "Even so, come, Lord Jesus."

From human perspective, no boy should have to grow up without a father. Words cannot express the sadness that clouded my life in those days that followed. It was the custom in those days to bring the embalmed corpse to the home awaiting the burial. Grief upon grief filled my heart, as I could peer into that open casket for two days. Kind friends and relatives would sit by the body throughout the night hours. It was called 'sitting up with the dead', a strange ritual indeed.

After the funeral service the sorrow was compounded as Mother insisted on going to the cemetery three and four times a week for a period of months, and I stood by her side as she wept out her grief. I can still remember telling her time and again, "Mother, Daddy is not here, he is with Jesus." Quite often I would vividly see him in a dream. Sometimes he would run to me and gather me up in his arms and assure me he was not dead, other times I would see him in a distant crowd and as I ran to him he would disappear. I would awaken with a pounding and broken heart.

After his death, Mother attended the Gospel Tabernacle often on Sunday nights. One night, Brother Tingley preached an energetic sermon on the Second Coming of Jesus. During the invitation I began to weep profusely as I pondered and longed for Him to return that very night. He had preached how that we would be reunited with our loved ones who had passed through the Veil of Death, and my heart was bursting with anticipation of seeing Daddy again. I will never forget a young boy, about my age, assuming I was under conviction, turning around and saying, "If you want to go forward and be saved, I'll go down the aisle with you." I could only respond by smiling and shaking my head. As we left the building that night, Mother and I wept together and I said, "Mother, wouldn't it be great if Jesus came back tonight?" Now, more than sixty years later, that is the plea of my heart, 'Even so, come quickly, Lord Jesus.'

Although my father had sold casualty insurance he had made little preparation for his own sudden death. After the funeral, little was left for the family's needs to be met. Mother immediately went to work and I found my first employment delivering the Birmingham Post Herald at the tender age of ten. We certainly were not people of poverty, but we were far from those of luxury. We never missed a meal, but we did eat a lot of beans and peas, tuna on toast and similar fare. Hand me down clothes, trips to the shoe shop for new half soles and heels, rather than a new pair, were the rule rather than the exception, but life was good and I doubt that few boys enjoyed growing up more than me.

Street hockey on roller skates, football in the street and on vacant lots, china berry battles with sling shots, Saturday double features, tag and chase in the dark of the night, competitive marble shooting and mischief in the neighborhood, best left without description. It was the best of times before T.V. and highly organized sports and I can honestly say no moments of boredom are lodged in my memory.

I truly feel sorry for kids today who must have their cell phones and are hooked on video games. They have never had the joy and excitement of finding four wheels off a discarded baby buggy, and absconding a few two-by-fours, and building their own go- cart. Oh, the thrill of speeding down the steep, hilly streets with the wind in your hair. Constructing you own skatey-mo, that's what we called them, built with an old pair of roller skates attached to a two-by-four with an upright board to steer the vehicle. Of course, you don't get the cuts and bruises or the skinned elbows and knees with the hand held videos, but those were our badges of honor.

POOR RICH KIDS

I do sense a certain melancholy, perhaps unwarranted, when I think of young boys who have never built a tree house, never searched for a green hickory limb, looking for that perfect branch shaped like the letter Y, cut two rubber strips from a discarded inner tube, removed the tongue from an old shoe and made a pocket for his prided slingshot. I wonder, do little boys ever pluck the white or yellow honeysuckle blossom, and gently pull the stem through the bottom of the flower to suck the one small drop of nectar? Gone forever are those days of sweet innocence, when Saturdays were given to certain chores, but longed for because it was the day of the double feature at the East Lake Theater where for twenty five cents one could spend half a day cheering you heroes, buy a bag of popcorn and have a nickel left over. The graphic, bloodletting scenes from the sewers of Hollywood today would bring loud howls of ridicule to the productions of yesteryear, but we were the better for it.

POOR ROLE MODELS

Just one block from our home was a very small grocery store, appropriately called "The Shack". Two WWII vets had bought the quaint enterprise and it became a sort of hang out for me. I was paid to sweep the floors and deliver groceries to nearby neighbors. One of the owners was a humble, soft-spoken, country fellow. His wife and parents, named Ma and Pa, aided him. The other partner was a raucous individual who felt it was his calling to introduce me to the facts of life. He was a likeable guy, but certainly not the best of characters to influence a ten-year-old boy.

A sketch of The Shack on 73rd Street and 2nd Avenue South.

Next door to the little grocery lived Uncle Heck and Aunt Lucile. They were not related to me or anyone else in the neighborhood; that was just their name. Uncle Heck had worked with my Dad and he daily frequented the Shack. He took me under his wing and became a second father to me. If I became ill at school I would go to Aunt Lucile's house until Mother got home from work. Many hours were spent in their home and countless meals were enjoyed there. I loved them and they loved me. I realize now that I was searching for someone to be a father figure.

Uncle Heck was a strong, robust man's man, one who loved hunting and fishing. From November until February we could be found in the woods of Double Oak Mountain, raccoon hunting. I was the little kid in tow with a bunch of old codgers scouring the steep hills and valleys in pitch black dark listening for the yaps and howls of a pack of Red Bone and Blue Tick canines, hot on the trail of a bandit faced raccoon. I can hear the proud owners now,
"That's ole' Blue or that's Loud" and then would ensue a heated argument, "No, #*&@, that's my Katie."

With carbide lanterns glowing, the clan would half trot towards the baying hounds until we stood at the foot of the treed four legged creature. I will not go into the gory details, but in the next few days to come, I would be sitting at Aunt Lucile's table, feasting on coon and sweet potatoes.

Many a Saturday morning we would emerge from the forest just before daylight and I would arrive home just in time to change clothes and be at work by 7:00 a.m. and labor until 7:00 p.m. As I look back at those escapades, I realize it was not the hunt I enjoyed, but it was the attempt to please and be accepted by Uncle Heck and the other men.

SKUNKED

One of those Saturday mornings, it was just before sunrise, we were making our way out of the woods, bouncing up a winding, rut filled logging road. I had been assigned to sit in the bed of the old pick up and instructed to hold the collars of two huge, weary hounds, lest they leap from the vehicle. As we bounced along, I was rocked to sleep by the motion of the swaying truck. Suddenly, I was awakened by the yelp of ole' Blue and he and Loud jerked themselves from my grip and over the side of the truck they went. They had caught the scent of a prey and caught the varmint about ten yards from the now stopped vehicle. To my shame and chagrin, it was not a coon nor possum, but a polecat, a skunk. I can't repeat the tongue-lashing I received from Uncle Heck, but my punishment was to secure those dogs till we were out of the woods.

Uncle Heck hardly spoke to me as we made our way back to Birmingham, but far worse was the retribution of the sickening stench of my clothes. When I finally arrived home and entered the house, Mother awoke and sent me back out on the front porch to strip down to my birthday suit. I had to scrub with Octagon Soap to remove the horrendous odor and she burned every stitch of clothes and my hunting boots.

I really came to love and admire Uncle Heck. He took me on many fishing trips, taught me how to rabbit and squirrel hunt, bought me my first shotgun, and gave me money to go to the State Fair when it came to Birmingham. Again, he was my adopted father. The negative aspect was that he was not the best role model. He introduced me to cuss words I had never heard and would blaspheme God without blinking an eye. I doubt there was a single day that he did not consume liquor and kept a five gallon keg of moonshine in his garage. I cringed at his swearing, but fortunately, never took up his habit of blaspheming God.

He had a daughter who finally married and gave birth to Heck's first grandson and, understandably, he became the apple of his eye. In my heart I became jealous when I found myself no longer number one in his life. For years he had promised that his twenty- gauge Winchester pump would be mine someday, but now the weapon was to be given to the grandson. Now as a father and granddad, I fully understand his decision, but then it was a crushing, gut wrenching experience. As a boy I felt betrayed and rejected and at that time in my life it was quite devastating. I began to harbor feelings of rejection.

CHAPTER 4

A BOY BEGUILED

A simple decision that was made for my welfare and benefit brought about a fairly drastic change of direction in my life. I have previously mentioned how my mother had to become the breadwinner shortly after the death of my father. She often worked fairly late at night and with my older brother also working I was left by myself quite often. We lived in a fairly large house with that huge coal-burning furnace in the basement and there were eerie noises suited to frighten a boy my age, and my vivid imagination compounded the situation. I can remember hearing suspicious sounds and creaking floors that caused my heart to pound, my blood run cold, that would drive me to crouch beneath a kneehole study desk with a loaded 38 revolver in my shaking hands, and the great relief I sensed when mother came home from work.

Mother during her working days.

Though I had no doubts about my salvation, I was far from sanctified and enjoyed mischievous pranks played out in the neighborhood. It is with chagrin when I hear older neighbors still recalling some of the incidents and labeling me the terror of the community. All things considered, Mother felt it would be best for me to go and live with my sister and her husband for part of each summer. The War was now over and Lynn, whom I called Tee Tee, (it seems that my older brother could not pronounce 'sister' and it came out 'Tee Tee,' and until the day she died, that was her name) lived in Ft. Worth in renovated army barracks in a government housing project. My sister, sixteen years my senior, really loved me, the baby of the family and I looked forward to and enjoyed the visits with her, my brother-in- law and their growing family.

At this time there remained a hunger in my heart for the will of God in my life. A church bus from the First Baptist Church came by the housing project each Sunday morning and carried us to Sunday school and worship service. My teacher was a young man named Dee Williams who had a heart for God and young boys. He gave me a Bible and was the first person to ever ask me if I was a Christian. The pastor was J. Frank Norris, a controversial and somewhat notorious, animated, loud and long-winded preacher, but he held my attention, which is a real compliment to him.

Each of these summers I would find some employment to make spending money. I helped a buddy with a large paper route, worked in a nearby grocery store and cut grass in the project. When I was eleven, a newfound friend in the housing project excitedly told me about a job opportunity where we could make big bucks at a local bowling alley as pinsetters. Of course this was before automation and our job would be to pick up the knocked down bowling pins, load them in a metal rack, ride it to the floor and roll the ball back down a wooden chute to the bowler. We were to be paid eleven cents a line plus tips that would be placed in the finger holes of the last ball thrown. With great pride I got my first Social Security card at age eleven and reported for duty, little realizing the pitfalls and temptations that I would encounter.

There were some liabilities to the job. Some sadistic bowlers delighted in tossing the second ball while pinsetters were still in the pit gathering knocked down pins from ball number one. A few times a bowling pin will be struck with force enough to fly up to the perch where we sat and bust your shins. But the most serious liability was not the physical, but the subtlety of the spiritual. My new occupation meant working till midnight on Saturdays and the need to be back at the alley by noon on Sunday and that meant no more church. Most of the guys who worked as pin-boys were tough kids. Fowl language, smoking, dirty jokes, gambling and beer drinking was the code of conduct. The ringleader was a muscular Mexican boy named Alonzo and for whatever reason he took a real liking to me. Lonzo, as we called him, would good naturedly pick on me and joke about my use of the terms, "Y'all" and "He'ah."

Most of my boyhood life I had been and was self-conscious about being small in frame. I had bought a set of weights and worked out nightly, practiced methods of muscular development by Charles Atlas, drank raw egg milkshakes, but with little success in improving by bony appearance. When Lonzo made me his buddy I experienced for the first time in my life a strong desire to fit in, to be accepted, to be a part of the crowd. Today it is called peer pressure and to me it was a genuine allurement and I found old Lucifer saying, "Hey, you don't have to be big to be big, just do what the big boys do."

And to my great shame and regret, I began to desire the favor of the guys more the favor of God. The big boys used fowl language and I made myself utter my first four letter swear word, they smoked and I puffed my first real cigarette and nearly coughed my head off and dared even to sip their beer.

There was a stinging in my heart and a misery that was to haunt me the next four years of my life, a misery that I later came to understand to have been the loving Father bringing conviction to a young boy who was beginning to rebel against His will for my life. So foolishly I thought to myself that I would soon be back in Birmingham and things would be different and no would one know what I had been doing, but He who loved me the most knew and I could not comprehend how much I was grieving His heart.

CHAPTER 5

CHOICES AND CONSEQUENCES

Through the years I often heard parents say when their kids rebelled, "Brother Bobby, he or she just got into the wrong crowd."

It is as if their children were innocent and without any blame. They ignore or fail to realize that the teenager chose his own companions and although there are certainly damaging influences, he or she made the willing choice. When I returned home I now found myself uncomfortable around those who walked in the light and more contented with those of darkness. That inner misery and restlessness still persisted deep in my heart, but there was also the longing to be accepted, to be in the so called 'in' crowd and to prove I was a 'man', whatever that means. Though there is no one else to blame, there was no spiritual challenge or encouragement in the home. To add to the rebellion of my own my heart was that of some very poor adult role models.

Prior to and during this time Mother had opened our home to roomers, fellows just back from WWII and mostly college students. Four guys stayed in two rooms hardly big enough to cuss a cat in and they each paid $20.00 a month. This required the relinquishment of my own bedroom and now not only did I have to share the bed with Bubba, we both had to sleep in mother's bedroom. When he became nineteen he joined the Air Force. I was only fourteen, but I would have joined the French Foreign Legion to escape having to sleep with him every night.

One of the roomers was George Valakes, who had recently been converted out of the Greek Orthodox Church. He was a ministerial student at Howard College and had a heart for God and souls. He would often carry me with him to a rescue mission near downtown Birmingham and would share his testimony and even ask me to play my dented second hand trumpet and brag on me as I hit about one note in ten. He gave me paperback books by D.L. Moody and was a real challenge to me. He was one of the few men who really took the time to encourage me toward Christ.

TROUBLE IN SCHOOL

When I entered the fourth grade at Barrett School we were required to enter a new class called 'Library.' I will not reveal the teacher's name, but will tell you she was the first person I can remember with blue hair. One could tell immediately that she was not the jolly green giant. On that first day, we were instructed to explore a particular area of the library and choose our first volume to digest. I paid no attention to the fact that all the other students had made their choice and I was still searching the shelves. Suddenly, someone snatched me up by the hair of my head, jerked me to an upright position and slammed a book into my chest. "Here's your book, go sit down and read it." I was angry and humiliated, and with reddened face I made my way to the table to sit down, midst the snickers and grins of other students. I vowed that day to get even with the blue haired witch, and for my remaining years of grade school, I searched for the time and the method to carry out my revenge.

**Graduation from Barrett School.
I'm the guy with the ears, front row, third from the right.**

D-DAY

Finally the day and opportunity came. Two of the college fellows who boarded in our home were pharmacy majors. Ray Ratliff brought home some concoction that would make rotten eggs smell like Evening In Paris. Just a few drops would clear a good-sized room in nothing flat. Just before graduation from grammar school, I plotted with a couple of friends how we could pay Old Lady So and So back for the misery she had caused all three of us. I would bring some of the Satanic, stinking solution to school and we would clandestinely pour the contents on some of her precious volumes. On arrival of that infamous day of destiny, I got cold feet. Hey, if I get caught, I won't be able to graduate. My buddies scoffed at my cowardice. Bobby L. said, "Give me the bottle and I will take it into the building," and Sammy agreed that he would do the dastardly deed. On the way to the third floor library, Sammy got cold feet, and decided to just pour the fowl potion down the open stair well, but tragedy of tragedies, as he uncorked the putrefying brew and began to pour it, some ran down on his arm. Bobby and I could lie our way out of the scheme, but not poor Sammy, he was branded.

School was dismissed early that day and the building emptied. As I pedaled my way home, I prayed that my involvement would not be discovered. Taking the remaining pint of the stinking solution, I hastened to the deepest point of the back yard and buried the evidence. As far as I know, it remains there till this day, some nearly sixty years later.

BE SURE YOUR SIN WILL FIND YOU OUT

About thirty minutes after arriving home, the telephone rang and I knew immediately I was caught. Mrs. Palmer, the school principle was on the other end of the line. Her words sent a chill down my spine. "Bobby, come to my office immediately." No explanation and none needed. No question or reply from me, I knew I was trapped. I don't know who ratted on me, but it made little difference because both Bobby and Sammy could whip me, and I did not dare threaten either of them. As I turned my bicycle onto Division Avenue at the school, I began to tremble.
There, parked in front of the building were two police cars and a number of people milling on the sidewalk. Mrs. Palmer and I had had a few other encounters, and I was not the apple of her eye. If looks could kill, and at that moment I wished they

could, better dead than face this music. They were not playing my song unless it was the funeral march.

Few young men have endured the tongue lashing I received that day. She was fit to be tied, as they say. We were threatened with the juvenile authorities and arrest. When I tried to lie my way out of the incident, Mrs. Palmer just increased the volume of her disgust with me and my fellow culprits. I was really convinced we were headed for the Boys Reform School, and I had watched enough of The Dead End Kids movies and the cruel Wardens at such institutions, to know that I was in more trouble than I ever wanted to find myself in.

It was a day of good fortune for me and my compatriots. The semester was ending, and Mrs. Palmer was being replaced by a new principle. His name was Mr. Bowie, a kind and gentle Christian gentleman who was coming from Woodlawn High School where he had served as Boys Advisor. He asked Mrs. Palmer if he could take me aside and talk with me. To my shame, I lied about my involvement and am confident he knew of my deceitful replies. Taking pity on me, and my buddies, he was satisfied with our suspension from school and no charges placed against us. (Many years later, I had the privilege of preaching a revival in his home church and asked his forgiveness for my fabrication and lying.) By now Mother had come to the school and when we got home, Mrs. Palmers haul over the coals was like a lullaby compared to Mother's rendition of rebuke.

HIGH SCHOOL DAYS

I entered Woodlawn High School in January of 1950. It was one of the so-called Big Five, being one of five largest high schools in the city. My four years there were still spent in rebellion to God's call upon my life. Mine was not a life of wickedness or immorality, but that of one seeking to be accepted. I believe that a number of incidents contributed to that longing for belonging. Silly things perhaps, but experiences that were and still are lodged in my psyche.

For one thing, it is often tough to be the little brother, especially when he is smarter, a better student and has a totally different personality. When I would enter a new class, the teacher would often remind me of Bubba's good grades and qualities. I can't explain it, but I have always had a mischievous streak and I could get in more trouble accidentally than he could on purpose. At home, when I disappointed Mother, she would compare me to my compliant sibling, and he was and has always been a good role model. Even as a boy, he was always generous and kind toward me. For whatever stupid reason, to me it brought resentment and a desire to rebel and be unlike him.

On the night of my father's death, I overheard my mother in conversation with a relative about our family. For the first time I learned that she had been married and divorced and that my sister was only my half sister. Someone mentioned that my sister was sixteen years older than me, and mother replied that I was an accident, an unplanned child. It sounds so ridiculous as I now write about it, but that revelation made me feel that I was an unwanted child.

As absurd as it must appear, these and other incidents brought about an attitude of resentment that developed an unjustified rebellion in my heart. In all of these conglomerations of incidentals, I feel sure that Old Slew foot, his Satanic Majesty, was chuckling in the background.

I am ashamed to admit the silliness of my craving for respect and acceptance. One of the more stupid adventures was to join up to box in the Golden Gloves. In the back of Cascade

Plunge, a somewhat famous swimming pool, a boxing ring had been set up and a man, Coach Thomas, agreed to try and train me. It did not take me long to realize there were better and easier ways to prove one's manhood. Rather than being a good boxer, I got boxed.

There were suspensions from school, coming home in the wee hours of the morning to a frantic and angry mother who was unable to control or restrain her son, two arrests warrants delivered to the door, and all in all, four wasted years of my life. In that time I saw my mother's hair turn from red to gray and more than once heard her bemoan that she could wish herself dead rather than face the torment I was bringing to her life. If ever there was a young rebel that needed a strong father to escort him to the basement and lay the board to his rear end and tell him to shape up or ship out, it was this ungrateful prodigal. Tough love is a necessity in every home and God's Word on the disciplining of a child is the best volume yet written. May He forgive us for adhering to a Dr. Spock mentality that has fostered generations of brats and bullies that now make the policies of a nation going to ruin.

To compound the regret of these delinquent years is the haunting realization that I could have had a positive witness for Jesus to my friends. Some, I have seen come to know Him as Lord and Savior, but most have scattered their separate ways, individuals who remind me of wasted opportunities. Bless the Lord that His forgiveness is complete, but the consequences of our iniquities remain.

CHAPTER 6

MASTERED BY THE MASTER

It was November in 1953. I was a senior about to graduate in January and I could hardly wait. So frustrated by the restraints and complaints at home, plans were in progress to join the Marines or Army as a paratrooper with some buddies. I was ready to get away from Mother so that nobody would tell me what to do or how to live my life, which proves how Satan can blind a young boy, and show him to be the fool he often is. But a gracious, Sovereign, loving God had other plans for His prodigal son.

Woodlawn High School permitted some guys and girls to start what they called Morning Watch. Twenty minutes before the first period they would gather, perhaps 100 students or more, in the school auditorium for times of devotional, testimonies or to hear a local pastor share. Of course I never attended lest someone consider me a religious wimp, but some fellows aroused my curiosity about an evangelist who was coming to speak. He was preaching a two-week revival at Central Park Baptist Church and I observed a definite change of lifestyle in some friends who had attended and made decisions in the first week of that Crusade. They began to pressure me about attending the services and finally I agreed to go with them, but only because of a desire to be with them rather than sit home alone, plus I felt after the service we would go out and do our thing.

It was with surprise that I viewed the huge church building as we entered the services and being late in a Baptist church meant the only seats left were down front. We were seated by ushers with a large number of other young people who were enthusiastically singing Christian choruses and when the evangelist walked onto the platform he was dressed in a sharp bright colored suit and I thought to myself, "Hey, this guy is different", and when he began to preach with real animation and humor, God began to speak to me. I cannot remember exactly what he preached, but I do know that when the invitation was extended the Holy Spirit so moved on my heart that I could feel the pounding in my chest, and I felt that I was the only person in that building. The evangelist, who later became a personal and treasured friend, asked those who sincerely wanted to get right with God to stand to their feet and as I stood, there was no regard for my friends around me or for the hundreds of others in that sanctuary. With tears and a pounding heart I stepped out into the aisle and made my way to the pastor of the church who stood at the front of the auditorium, and as best I could phrase, I told him that I wanted "to get right with God."

The evangelist, Eddie Martin from Pennsylvania, led me and about two dozen others back to a room for counseling. He gave each person, who had come forward a red, paperback Gospel of John and carefully explained how to be saved and how a saved person who had rebelled could come back into fellowship with his Savior. After leading us in a prayer of confession and repentance, I left the room to go and join my friends. I can still remember walking out in the crisp November night air and seeing the bright moon shining through the leafless trees and I felt that my feet touched the ground about every three yards. Never had there been such a relief from guilt and the sensation that a burden had literally been lifted from my shoulders. Amazingly, I felt the acceptance I had so longed for through those years of rebellion and there was now a desire to embrace the call God had placed on my heart as a ten-year old boy.

My friends were waiting for me, and joy filled the car as we drove to the Tel-Hop restaurant on old Hwy. 78, to get our burgers and fries and discuss what had happened that night. It was nearly midnight when I got home, and for the first time in almost four years I didn't try to slip in the house that night in order to miss the grueling third degree from Mother. I would pull off my shoes and tiptoe in. I even squirted graphite in the keyhole of the front door, trying to silence clicks of the lock, but never succeeded in making a silent entrance. But this night was different.

Opening the front door and calling out to her she walked into the hallway groaning out, "What have you done now?" Sitting down in the living room, I told her that I was not leaving home after graduation, but that I had recommitted my life to the Lord and was now going to college and preach God's Word. I made my way back to my little bedroom and began to read the red Gospel of John I had received that night. Suddenly, God's Word came alive and I knelt beside the bed to thank God for what He had done in my life. I slept little that night and repeated the reading and praying through the night. November 3, 1953, a night to never be forgotten!

CHAPTER 7

CRAVING FOR THE CLASSROOM

It is a sorry admission, but true, other than being with my friends, I hated school but when Mother rapped on the door the next morning I sprang out of bed like a little kid on Christmas. Never had there been such an anticipation to get to old Woodlawn High and tell all who would listen about my new found joy and the person of Jesus, with an unbelievable desire to see them come to know Him. Back in those days it didn't take fifteen minutes to get ready for school. Rush to the bath room, throw some water on your face, slap the Brylcreem on your hair and comb your 'ducktails' in place, slip into the tee shirt, hitch up your too tight jeans, pull up the crew socks and lace up the blue suede shoes and you were cool, and ready for the day.

Striding up the steps and turning to the left, I took my place by the trophy cases of past school heroes, where all the jocks gathered to shoot the breeze. Like a fellow that had just struck his first hole in one or a bass fisherman who had caught a ten pounder, I could not contain myself, but had to share what I "had seen and heard," but most of all, had experienced. Expecting the guys to say how great that was and tell me how they wanted the same, I was somewhat surprised when Billy Mac looked me in the eye and with cynical sarcasm replied, "Britt, it won't last two weeks. I'll betcha' five bucks in two weeks you will be just like you were, doing the same things, cussing and ...."

Rather than being a discouragement to me it became a challenge to prove him wrong, knowing that I would be under his and other's scrutiny and surveillance. (By the way, it didn't last, it got better and better and fifty plus years later it is better than ever! How did that lost, spiritually ignorant guy know that?)

I was never the most attentive student in the classroom, but that day was worse than any. My mind was constantly on going back to the revival service, almost twenty miles across the city, and as the service was anticipated and envisioned, I did not see the evangelist preaching, but I saw *me* standing in the pulpit sharing with all what God had done in my heart and life. In my almost misdirected enthusiasm I hit guys and girls up for money to give an offering to that preacher that the Lord has used to bring joy unspeakable to my empty soul.

The following night our Student Body President, and also the leader of the Morning Watch services, had the evangelist and Music evangelist come to his home after the service and meet with about twenty of us, a number who had made decisions in the Crusade. He graciously shared with us and challenged us and I proudly gave him the "love offering" lifted from fellow students. It was a night of special encouragement and the beginning of a friendship that was to grow with the years, as in time to come, I would be considered a fellow evangelist.

MY FIRST SERMON

The following week I was asked to speak to the Morning Watch assembly, and though excited and humbled at the opportunity, I was scared out of my wits. By the time of the appointed hour I had read from the New Testament book of Romans and chose as a text, "For I am not ashamed of the Gospel of Christ." I had liberty beyond my fondest imagination even though Mr. Martin, the school principle, was in the audience that day. To me it was an affirmation that our Lord did indeed want me to preach His Word, and now, I looked forward to graduation with a new incentive, not to just get out of school, but to get into school, a college that He could use to better prepare me for His call upon my life.

A LESS THAN ENTHUSIASTIC RESPONSE

The following Sunday I attended Sixty-Sixth Street Baptist Church where I had made public my profession of faith and was baptized at age nine. Walking down the steps following the service I turned to go back into the auditorium. My memory still carries the picture of standing in the aisle beneath the balcony and announcing to our pastor that I felt that God was calling me to preach. Never to be forgotten was the shock written on his face as he spontaneously chuckled and blurted out, "You?" Had it not been for the problems I had caused for Sunday school teachers and my inattention and whispering during his sermons, I might have been disappointed, but it also became another incentive and challenge to prove him wrong in the days to come.

I would be less than honest if I did not admit that some sadness followed those fresh days of newfound excitement. There came an uncomfortableness around most of my old buddies. Now when they cursed it would pierce my heart and smutty jokes made me feel dirty. Few experiences grieved me as much as seeing a friend drinking a bottle of beer one night. It was especially heart breaking, because he too had made a decision in that same revival meeting, and we had planned to team up, he was to sing and I was to preach. I went home that night with tears in my eyes and a deep sense of loneliness. I honestly believe that I was not expressing the attitude of a Pharisee, but God had put in my spirit a new sensitivity not only to my own sin but that of others.

CHAPTER 8

COLLEGE DAYS

January 1954, the long anticipated night had arrived, graduation from high school and the days of no more school, no more books and exams and demanding teachers, ah, what relief and how relished was the idea. And yet, here I was looking forward to college and preparation for His call upon my life. Just weeks after graduation I enrolled at Howard College, a liberal arts, Baptist supported institution and only four blocks from home. Soon to be discovered was that my expectations were somewhat exaggerated in that I expected the institution to be a Bible School with a total Christian environment, safe from the world, a place of hallowed ground and ultra conservative theology. In the Religion Department were some of the most Godly men I have ever known but there were a few that were to challenge my simple faith and spiritual immaturity. When professors used terms like "Patriarchs," "Divinity" "Deity", "The Divided Kingdom," etc, I didn't have a clue, but was too embarrassed to ask. I was not quite as ignorant as the fellow who thought that an epistle was the wife of an apostle, but almost.

In this new setting, I met and developed some lifelong friendships. God provided fellows my same age that had a deep love for Christ and a solid commitment to Him and His Kingdom. Of special challenge were some older guys, WWII and Korean War vets, that had surrendered to the ministry, who took me under wing and fellowshipped with me.

One of these fellows was Daryl Jones from Leeds, Alabama. He had been a successful businessman, a veteran of WWII, had lived a sorted lifestyle and only recently come to know Jesus as his Lord and Savior. Daryl was in his early thirties, had three children and his wife had died in an automobile accident a few months before. We both shared a deep sense of God's call upon our lives, a hunger to see people saved and a passionate love for bass fishing. These qualities were to bring us into a long and sustained bond in Christ. His challenge to my personal life will be mentioned later.

OPENING DOORS OF OPPORTUNITY

Tent Revival in Birmingham

Howard College had a program for ministerial students called H-Day, whereby Baptist Associations throughout the state would invite preacher boys to fill the pulpits of participating churches. A list would be posted in Old Main and fellows desiring to preach would sign up. Assignments would be made with the more experienced guys going to the larger churches and the new or lesser experienced to the smaller fellowships. It was with trembling hand and heart that I placed my name on the list to go to the Walker County Association in the spring of 1954 and a few days later see that I was to speak at the Goodsprings Baptist Church the following Sunday. It was one of the larger churches, and because there was another

Bobby Britt, older than myself, who had served as a pastor, I was accidentally placed there. About twenty of us arrived at the First Baptist Church in Jasper and met those who were to take us to the several fellowships. Nathan Groves, a deacon of the church, introduced himself and proceeded to drive me to the location. Green as grass and still wet behind the ears, as the expressions go, we made our way down the country roads to the destination. As we drove along, we passed various Baptist Churches. As I read the identifying signs, I asked, "What is a Primitive Baptist Church.... what is a Missionary Baptist...a Freewill Baptist...an Independent Baptist Church?" All of these labels were new to me and I could tell he was somewhat astonished at my ignorance. I feel sure that he was apprehensive about letting this young squirt preach in his church. We finally arrived at Goodsprings Baptist Church. I was shocked to see the size of the auditorium and the number of autos parked outside, though it is doubtful that more than a hundred people were in attendance.

It would be difficult to describe the terror that filled the heart of that eighteen-year-old preacher-boy as I waited the time to stand in the pulpit, read my text and sermonize. Likewise it would be impossible to explain the sudden energy and freedom that immediately came and the sense that I could hardly move my lips rapidly enough to express the thoughts that flooded my mind. It was almost like an out of the body experience and our loving Lord again confirmed to my heart, that indeed He had called me to preach His Word and that His hand was upon a young man's seeking heart.

God used those days and the H-Day program to open many future doors with opportunities for youth meetings and revivals for years to come, and it is with gratitude and thanksgiving that I can attest to the fact that I was privileged to see hundreds of people coming to make open confessions of Jesus as Savior and Lord. I recently spoke in a church where a man introduced himself and told me how that he and seven other people had accepted Jesus nearly fifty years before during those college days.

A LIFE TIME DREAM

Days at Howard College were not just about preaching and fellowship. As long as I can remember, I always longed and dreamed of playing football. As mentioned earlier, the death of my Dad necessitated my need to begin some sort of work if I wanted spending money. The paper route at age ten, a pin boy at eleven, working in a grocery store as stock boy, check out and bag boy, produce department, helping in the meat market, sweeping floors, you name it and I did it, all for about forty cents an hour. Two summers I was a curb boy at the famous Spinning Wheel or The Polar Bear. It was an iconic place in Birmingham, built like a giant igloo with polar bears adorning the roof- top.

The Polar Bear or The Spinning Wheel

Although I never felt deprived by having to work through grade and high school, I guess I resented not being able to go out for football. But as a freshman college student the door did open. I learned that Howard was to travel to Mexico City to play The University of Mexico in the fall of 1954. That summer I worked for a construction company the weeks I was not preaching. I saved every dime I possibly could and by the end of August I had hoarded seven hundred dollars. Bobby Bowden, who was to become famous as the coach of Florida State University, was an assistant and became my coach.

These were the years following the end of the Korean War and a number of the guys were now in college on the G. I. Bill. I weighed about 160 pounds, had not played in high school, and needless to say spent most of my football career on the bench, but I did get to go to Mexico, made all the trips with the team and got to eat steaks with all the first stringers. It really did fulfill a lifelong desire and believe it or not, past three-score and ten, I still have vivid dreams of being back on the gridiron. Of course, my dreams are filled with only athletic success.

In the years that followed, I have had the opportunity to develop a friendship with Coach Bowden. He returns to Birmingham almost every summer and plays golf with his old buddies. I am privileged to participate in a few of those rounds of golf. On a couple of occasions, Bobby has accepted the invitation to speak in churches where I was either pastor or interim pastor. I jokingly introduce him as one of the best coaches in America, but observed he has a short memory. When I played for him at Howard College, in the mid fifties, I played defensive and offensive end. I tell how I would come off the bench and plead, "Coach, let me go in," to which he would answer, "Get your tail back on that bench." I joke that he forgot I was an end and not a tail back.

55th Reunion of 1953-54 Football Team with Coach Bobby Bowden

CHAPTER 9

REVIVAL FLAMES

The fall of 1955 was the beginning of a new era for my life. Perhaps it had been the influence of the evangelist that God had used to turn my life around, but for whatever reason, my deepest desire was to serve the Lord as an evangelist. That longing constantly burned in my heart. One night, Joe Crumpler, the pastor of a small church in a coal mining community, called inviting me to preach an eight-day revival and I gladly accepted. Joe was a WWII veteran who worked with my mother, attended college at night and was the pastor of Empire Baptist Church in Walker County. It was a week never to be forgotten. Coal miners, by in large, have a culture all their own. Dirt roads, well water, outhouses, the Company Store where "clacker" was used rather than cash, tough men and also some of the finest folks who were the salt of the earth.

I rode with the pastor each night to the meeting and we met in a white frame building with a glowing pot bellied stove that sat right in the middle of the sanctuary. At least once during each service, Lamar, a precious mentally challenged young man, would make his way to that sole source of heat, shake out the ashes with a banging, clanging reverberation and load fresh coal to the fire.

By Tuesday night the building was filled but no one had come forward to receive Jesus as Savior and my heart was burdened. I groaned in my spirit that night and cried out to God asking why not a person had been saved. As the last few people were leaving the service, and we were about to make the drive back to Birmingham, a teenage boy stepped out of the dark and spoke to me asking if I would pray with him as he asked the Lord Jesus to be his Savior. Gene Cagle, a name to never be forgotten, told me how he had walked home, but could not enter the house and was compelled by deep conviction, returned to settle things with a Holy God. He was the first convert in a ministry of evangelism that was to be blessed for more than thirty years. He later became a successful Methodist minister.

At the close of the eight days, forty-nine people had walked the aisle to make Jesus Lord and Savior and a number of those were adult miners for whom wives, children, the community and the church had prayed for years. Mr. Dunn, seventy year old, gave his heart to Jesus that week. Bless the Lord for the continuing confirmation that I was where He wanted me to be and doing what He wanted me to do.

THE WORD OF GOD'S BLESSING SPREADS

Shortly after the meeting at Empire Baptist, word spread to other surrounding communities and invitations were extended to preach in other mining areas and the Lord graciously blessed the preaching of His Word. In one small church in the northern part of Birmingham the pastor baptized 92 people after an eight-day meeting. Before long invitations were coming from all over the state and I found myself driving often over a hundred miles after classes, returning home in the wee hours of the morning, for a few hours of sleep, and barely enough study, but youth feels itself invincible, and sad to say, I felt that grades were secondary as long as I made passing grades. Summer months were packed with as many as six successive weeks of preaching every night and most of the meetings had weekday services scheduled Monday through Friday.

AN ATMOSPHERIC REVIVAL

Atmospheric revival, I had never heard the term until Manley Beasley used that description to describe the Spirit of God falling on an entire community in such a way that one could almost feel His Presence.

Only once have I been privileged to participate in such an occurrence. I was twenty years old and was invited to preach a revival at the Fortieth Avenue Baptist Church. It was the spring of 1956. The church was located in a typical blue-collar area of North Birmingham. It was a small fellowship of perhaps 150 people. From the very first service, it was evident that His Hand was on the meeting. A godly young man, Ken Spears, led the singing and I did the preaching. The church building had a small bell tower steeple, in which were mounted two loudspeakers. Each afternoon, about an hour before the services began, the pastor, Clayton Lee, asked Ken and me to speak to the surrounding homes by means of those loudspeakers. Ken, not a great vocalist, would sing a verse or two of a hymn and I would speak for a few minutes, sharing the gospel.

One night a husky ironworker came forward to give his heart and life to Jesus. He related how he was getting out of his car and walking toward the house, when he heard the message, was stopped in his tracks and prayed to receive Jesus. Another night, a wife and mother told how she was washing supper dished at the sink, the kitchen window was open and the Holy Spirit brought such conviction, she bowed her head in repentance and received Jesus as Lord and Savior. At the conclusion of the eight day meeting the pastor reported that he baptized ninety-two people as they came and trusted Jesus as Savior. The blessed Holy Spirit just seemed to take up residence in the neighborhood.

I stood amazed as God blessed every revival meeting with souls coming to Jesus and now some fifty years later am more amazed that He would use a young man who really knew so little about the Lord whom He preached.

GOD SENDS A HELPMATE

Our Wedding, June 1, 1956

It was during this time that I had met a young girl with whom I would fall in love and later marry. Carolyn Maxwell and I had attended high school together, but we had never met. I had gone to Panama City, Florida with some old friends and they began to party, and in my aggravation with them, I left their companionship and also my place to sleep in the process. Knowing that some sorority girls from Woodlawn High were having a house party nearby, I humbly bargained with one of the housemothers to let me wash dishes for them, if they would let me sleep on the front porch of the beach house. A lovely young girl felt sorry for the beach bum and was willing to share her food with me. On Sunday night a friend and I made plans to attend a little storefront church and Carolyn and her friend asked if they could go with us. After fifty years of marriage I still joke and say that she asked me for our first date and her reply is she thought there was a large group planning to go and it really had nothing to do with me, but I know better. I hitched a ride back to Birmingham and our continuing courtship grew to engagement and in the spring of 1956 we were married.

This proved to be one of the best decisions I ever made and much more will be shared in pages to follow. But let me add a word of warning to all young folks contemplating taking the nuptial vows, you had better carefully consider that sacred pledge, "for better, for worse, in sickness and in health."

BECOMING A PASTOR

About a year after our marriage the Maytown Baptist Church, a small community just a few miles out of Birmingham, extended a call to me to come as pastor. One of the requirements in becoming a pastor was that of a formal ordination service. This was accomplished by having your home church, mine being the Sixty-Sixth Street Baptist fellowship, call an examining board of local ordained men to examine the doctrinal views held by the young candidate and to ask any questions they desired or deemed necessary.

"When were you saved?' "How do you know that you are called to preach?" Tell us how you would lead a soul to Jesus?"

As the questions proceeded, I was as nervous as a long tail cat in a room of rocking chairs. On and on the inquiry preceded until one of the more elderly gentleman cleared his throat, requested the floor and stated he must ask me one of the most important questions. A Holy hush gripped the room and he faced me eyeball to eyeball, clearing his throat a final time, he queried me, asking, "Brother Bobby, tell us the difference in eternal life and everlasting live." I stumbled for some moments and finally admitted that I saw no difference. With firm rebuke, he commented that 'eternal life' was what God had and enjoyed, but everlasting life is that given to us at salvation and was therefore quite different from God's eternal life. First, there was a restless murmuring among the dozen or so examiners and the voices grew angry and disagreeable. All of the attention now centered on the aged examiner and now ensued a hot debate among all the preachers, and thus concluded my Ordination Service and I must admit it was completed with my great relief.

NEW ADVENTURE

Maytown Baptist Church was a sweet fellowship of about fifty or sixty people and although my heart still beat for evangelism, I was impressed that this was the will of God for us at that time. They offered us a salary of $40.00 per week and a parsonage next door to the church. It had three bedrooms and a path to an outhouse, a two seater. Because of underground mining, the well had gone dry and every drop of water had to be hauled in a five-gallon jug or caught at a downspout. I could shower at school after P.E. class, but we would drive a few miles to Bro. Bob's house, which did have a well, and Carolyn would tuck her knees and climb into a number two washtub and take her bath. As a preacher, I was excited at the challenge, but for Carolyn it was more than just a step of faith. Having been raised in a well to do home, a mother who was a genteel lady and a fastidious Southern Bell, well, it was to be a real adjustment. But I can honestly say there were few words of complaint. Who can blame a petite, city-slicker girl for being a little uneasy about brushing your teeth with a pail of water, while standing on the back porch in full view of motorists passing by, thirty feet away, and some honking their horns? Shouldn't there be some reluctance to pull a potty from under the bed when nature calls at two o'clock in the morning and it's twenty degrees outside and the outhouse is fifty feet away? But in all of this I cannot remember one word of protest or grumbling. She was and is a real trooper.

TWEETIE BIRD

One night, we ventured to Bro. Bob's for Carolyn's Saturday night bath before Sunday morning church. The tub was brought into the kitchen, filled with water and we waited while the submerged electric heater warmed the water. The family and I sat in the living room as Carolyn made her way back to the kitchen. As we chatted we suddenly heard a blood-curdling scream. Rushing to my sweet wife's aide, she cried, "Someone is at the window and just whistled at me." Enraged, I ran out the door to catch the culprit that had so invaded her privacy. Finding no one, I reentered the house and found the family in hilarious laughter. The whistling peeping tom was only the pet parakeet, doing what little birds do, whistle. To this day, I am convinced that Carolyn was gravely disappointed.

Not realizing it, we were as "pore as Job's turkey" and as happy as if we had good sense. We were not embarrassed to place two apple crates against the wall, lay some boards across the top, put up a mirror, hang some curtains across the front and call it a dresser.

Two college buddies were invited to assist us in revival services. Max would lead the singing and Ned would display his gifts and talents as a chalk artist. The two shared a bed in one of the bare bedrooms and sometime in the middle of the night, there was a loud crushing thud, and we scrambled to see the bed and mattress had suddenly collapsed under the stress of their rotund torsos, and they were lying on the bare floor. The following morning, as were saying the blessing for breakfast, the four legs on Ned's chair began to creak and groan, and then abruptly went in four different directions, creating a fearsome scene as we saw our household furniture being destroyed by degrees.

We saw the largest number of people saved that year than the church had seen for a long time and the sweet gracious people put up with a young preacher who had a great deal of zeal, but I am sorry to say, without much knowledge. Added to my lack of pastoral skills was the fact that I unwittingly was away too often preaching revivals in other churches and yet to this day people are still complimentary of those blessed days at Maytown. A little over a year later we resigned to go back into evangelism and began to pray about where we were to attend seminary.

THE GLORY DAYS

Those four years of college days and preaching opportunities are looked back upon with absolute amazement as I consider the gracious hand of God upon our lives. Television was still in its infancy, organized Little League sports had not come on the scene, most wives were still homemakers and the Church was the central place of interest and activity. It was not an attitude of legalism, but just a sense of loyalty to a local fellowship. When a revival was announced, the people would set aside the date and most often the church buildings would be filled to capacity. Driving a little 1951 Studebaker thousands of miles to small country churches and some large, unsuspecting fellowships, really knowing so little about life and the Word of God, sadly lacking proper reverence and respect for some of the pastors with whom I served, and their patience with a young strutting youth evangelist. And yet in spite of all the deficiencies and failures of those earliest years, literally hundreds of people were saved, often churches were filled beyond capacity, revival meetings were extended to extra days and there were many times when the Glory of God was so evident one could literally sense and know His dynamic presence. The time of invitation would sometimes last for half an hour or more as we sang, "Oh, Why Not Tonight," "Don't Go Away Without Jesus," "There Is Room At The Cross For You," and other blessed hymns of invitation. It can only be attributed to abundant Grace, Mercy and Patience.

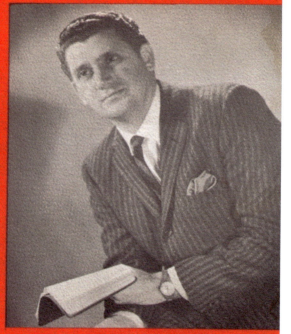

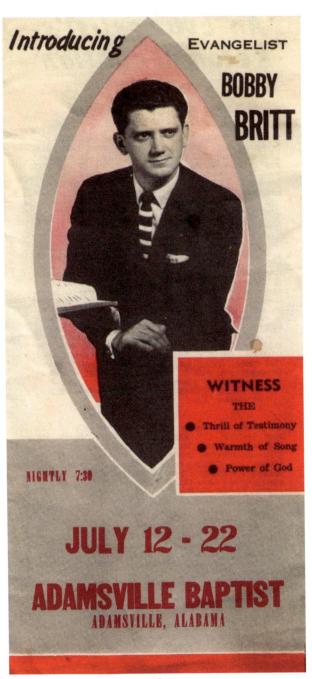

CHAPTER 10

MEMORABLE MOMENTS
(NOT TOO SPIRITUAL)

I could write a short novel about some of the places I have lodged during my travels as an evangelist and some of the things I have eaten, or tried to. Don't accept these shared experiences as ingratitude and certainly not as mockery of the people involved, just some things that came as a surprise, and sometimes shock, to a young city slicker preacher.

LIVESTOCK IN THE HOUSE

On one particular occasion I was invited to preach in a little country church and then invited home to eat with one of the families. Arriving at the residence I noticed it was a literal log house, not the kind we see today, built from a prepackaged kit. It was a house constructed out of logs, hewn in the local wooded area. To go into the domain, one had to stoop because of the low doorframe. We were immediately ushered to the table with a vinyl tablecloth and loaded with country delicacies. The only drink of choice was a large glass of milk that was dipped from a milk churn in the hallway. As I was enjoying my meal, I heard someone slurping their beverage and turning to see who the uncultured derelict might be, I cringed when I observed a hound dog with his head down in the churn lapping the milk with enthusiasm. The host stomped his foot and screamed, "Git out of here," and with a yelp the mongrel tucked his tail and fled out the door. Some minutes later, noticing my glass was nearly empty, he asked, "Preacher, you want some more milk?" With all the politeness I could muster, I replied, "No sir," and gagged down the rest of my meal.

"HOW DO YOU LIKE CHLILDREN?"
W.C. FIELDS REPLIED, "FRIED."

Many, many of the meetings I preached in those days were in small country churches and because motels could not be found or afforded, I made my abode in the homes of church members. That usually meant that some family member had to sacrifice his or her bedroom with the intruder. A number of homes had no closets and dressers were already filled with clothes of others. I lived for eight days out of suitcase on the floor and my suits were hung on a nail on the back of a door. I shared the same bathroom with the whole family and it seemed the clan grew each day. In the country setting, most folks got up with the chickens, but that was not my custom. As a young buck, I could hang with the best until two o'clock in the morning, but seven a.m. was an early time to rise. More than once I awakened to see two little beady eyes staring at me and hear the young delinquent holler, "Hey, Momma, he is still in the bed." Oh, the humiliation and the desire to wring his dirty little neck.

HEARTBREAKING DILEMMA

One of the saddest experiences was that of an invitation to eat with a family who were the poorest of tenant farmers. It was the custom, in most instances, not only have the noon meal, but to also return to the same home and have supper. (You high falooten folks call that dinner, that's what we eat at midday. Even Jesus told the parable of the supper, not the diner. I think I'll go along with Jesus.) As the pastor and I drove down the rutty dirt road, we stopped in the yard of the board and batten house, that could be best described as a shack. We brushed aside a couple of skinny hound dogs and a yard full of chickens and stood at the open door of the dwelling.

Immediately a frail, pregnant lady, with a child on her hip, graciously invited us in and straightway sat us her table. There were no screens on the open widows, back and front doors stood open and it was a hot, hot day in South Alabama. Hens and roosters were allowed to enter the house and chicken droppings spotted the floor. Little fare was on the table and the main meal was field peas and cornbread. As I sat there, I noticed at least a dozen flies in formation with their heads feasting on the juice that covered the peas. When I served myself, I dipped the spoon as quickly as I could in the bottom of the bowl, trying to avoid the contamination of the insects.

As difficult as it was, I could not embarrass the pastor or gracious hostess by eating nothing. As we left the house and made our way to the pastor's auto, I told him that there was no way I could return for the evening meal and preach that night. Clifford returned to the lady, still standing in the doorway and offered some excuse and not only was I relieved, but I felt she shared the same sentiment.

My heart still aches as I recall the incident, the poverty of the family, the hospitality revealed and my inability to face the dire situation.

SLEEPING IN THE FUNERAL HOME

Without a doubt, my most memorable place of lodging was in a small town in Oklahoma. The local funeral director and his family were members of the First Baptist Church of Walters. The town provided no decent motels or hotels, but the friendly undertaker had built a guest room on the end of the funeral home, adjacent to the office. If you can use your imagination and picture the configuration of the structure, try to envision a long building, L shaped on both ends. On one extreme of the edifice, the working area was located, and then a garage area that housed the hearses and family autos separating the family's residence which was located at the other end of the building. Each night it was my privilege to come to my room after the revival services, change into comfortable clothes, and wind my way through the eerie chambers that housed the casket viewing rooms, past the embalming room and counseling chambers, through the garage area, and then to dine with the family.

As fate would have it, one night I became confused in the almost darkened hallway and opened the door to find myself standing beside the corpse of a naked, elderly female. With adequate haste, I fled the scene and never made the mistake of losing my way the rest of the week.

READ AT YOUR OWN RISK

On a particular, unforgettable occasion, Carolyn and I were graciously invited into a home for the noon meal. The house was neat, the food was delicious and the fellowship enjoyable. At the conclusion of the repast, Carolyn offered her services to help put away the leftovers and to wash the dishes. Putting on an apron, she was led to the sink, and was instructed to use the dishrag that was draped on the faucet. Her eyes nearly popped out of their sockets when she discovered the dishrag was a pair of ladies panties! To say that she was shocked would be the understatement of the decade.

CULTURE DICTATES THE MENU

It did not take many years for me to discover that where you were often determined what you ate. For instance, I preached a meeting in a Southern part of Texas known as the angora capital of the world. And proud of it they were. Because angora is gathered from goats, that was the meat of choice to feed the young preacher from Alabama. Day after day, it was BBQ goat, baked goat, roasted goat, goat stew, goat, goat, goat and more goat. I feared I would soon eek goat odor and stand up to preach and say, "Baaaaaaa!"

THE PERSIMMON PUCKER

Preaching up in the northern corner of Illinois grew some of the largest persimmons I had ever seen. In Alabama we have plenty of what we consider 'possum chow', but they are hardly larger than a small crab apple. But these suckers were the size of a healthy peach and they were the pride of the county. Almost every home I entered served persimmons, persimmon salad, persimmon cobbler, persimmon cake. The worst part was that the fruit was bland and tasteless. The apostle Paul said, "eat what is set before you, asking no questions," but I doubt he had ever encountered a persimmon.

THINGS ARE NOT ALWAYS AS THEY APPEAR

In the fellowship of the first church I served as pastor was a dear sweet lady who would put Betty Crocker to shame. Believe me; you have never really eaten fried chicken until you dined at Sister Wilder's table. But, if there was one other cuisine that even topped the skillet-fried fowl, it was her fresh strawberry cobbler. Crusted on the bottom and the top, it would make you 'want to slap your grandmaw' as the ole redneck southerner would say. When we moved away from the Maytown church field, I could only dream of finding a cobbler equal to Sister Wilder's. But bless the Lord, some years later Carolyn and I were invited to dine in a little country home. As we entered the kitchen and sat down for the meal, I nudged Carolyn and nodded my head toward a beautiful double-crusted cobbler with slits in the top layer of dough and beautiful, luscious red juice was seeping through the cover. With glee, I whispered, "Strawberry Cobbler." It was so stunning, the sin of lust welled up in my heart. So anxious to gratify my taste buds, I nervously thought, 'why don't you folks stop talking, take away our plates and serve the dessert?' Finally, the cobbler was placed in the center of the table and the hostess was kind enough to let the visiting preacher scoop out the first portion, and digging deep and long I plunged the spoon into the longed for treasure. I waited a few moments while the lesser saints were served and with appropriate glee, I lifted the tablespoon of heaven to my mouth. For a moment I sat there shocked, amazed and sadly disappointed. I was not sure what it was, but it definitely was not strawberry pie. As I gagged and now wondered how do I get this gluttonous amount of red gook off my plate, our hostess looked at me and asked, "Well, Bro. Bobby, how do you like my very own tomato cobbler?" With my mouth full, I knew I could not spit it out, I could only nod my head and say, "Umh, Umh." Translated it meant, "Awful."

A SHOCK TO THE CITY SLICKER

I never thought of myself as living a sheltered life, pretty well exposed to all manner of lifestyle. That misleading evaluation became clear while preaching in a little country church. The building was filled to capacity, every seat was taken and a young mother sat on the very front pew holding an infant in her arms. I had some reservation that the little child would become restless, disturbing to me and those in the pew. I must admit that I was too preoccupied with their presence. In the midpoint of the message, the mother began unbuttoning her blouse and with absolute exposure proceeded to nurture her little one. It was not with impure imaginations filling my mind, but it was with sincere shock I observed a scene I had never witnessed before. No other person seemed to even give it a glance, but it was a new experience for a sheltered, city slicker preacher boy.

CHAPTER 11

OFF TO SEMINARY

The year of 1958 was one of new beginnings. I had graduated from Howard College and early in the year we had joyfully learned that Carolyn was pregnant and our firstborn would arrive in late August or early September, and that would be perfect timing. We had prayed and were impressed that we should enroll at Southwestern Baptist Theological Seminary in Ft. Worth, Texas in mid September. I had a terrifically busy schedule of meetings all spring and summer. The time for delivery came, but the baby didn't. First, anxious days and then weeks. What to do? Few meetings had been scheduled because of plans to enter seminary and to miss September enrollment meant a wait until January. After much prayer and with the encouragement from Carolyn, I loaded our belongings in a 5x8 U Haul and began the trek to Ft. Worth alone, trusting the Lord and Carolyn's mother to care for her. I was confident that when the anticipated long distance call came a flight would be available to get me back to Birmingham in time to share in the excitement.

A few days later enrollment day came. As I went through the process of being admitted and signing up for classes a sudden sense of loneliness swept over me. Though a half dozen couples from Alabama joined me in this new venture, I suddenly realized I knew not one pastor in the whole of Texas and worse than that, no one knew me and that was a blow to my ego. The years of youth meetings and revivals had brought some fair amount of name recognition and I am so ashamed to admit that I rather enjoyed it and now just a face in the crowd. This was a much needed humbling experience.

My older brother, Frank, and his wife Edna, who lived in Ft. Worth, invited me to stay with them until I could locate an apartment near the seminary. On the morning of September 22nd we were awakened by the noisy jangle of the telephone with the welcomed news that Carolyn was on the way to the hospital to give birth to our first-born. With unusual haste, the suitcase was packed and I made a beeline to Carter Field for the next available flight to Birmingham. Begrudging each of the four intermediate stops of the Delta DC6 we finally arrived to be met by Carolyn's mom to learn she was the new grandmother of her first grandson. It is still debatable as to who was the most proud. The joy was somewhat dulled when I learned that Carolyn had experienced a terrifically difficult delivery due to a breech birth and an old fashioned physician with poor bedside manner who didn't believe in adequate anesthesia. Rapidly the next several days flew by and I returned to Ft. Worth but not before taking Carolyn to her parent's home and with Robert Daniel Britt cradled in my arms.

Arriving back at seminary I struggled to catch up on missed class work, search for a place to live and explore the classified ads to purchase some used furniture. Two weeks later, weeks that seemed like months, I met Carolyn and Danny at the airport and with tremendous excitement made our way to our little three-room duplex at 1000 West Waggoman. I was so proud of how the new home had been furnished and Carolyn bragged on my purchases and the how adequately I had placed everything and put the linens, utensils, flatware, Mel Mac (that is, dishes to you less than old folks) until she questioned me about the small plastic handled sponge mop on the kitchen counter. She shrieked with horror when I explained it was the instrument I used to wash the kitchenware as it was unpacked and to wash the daily dishes until she arrived. It was then my time to shriek when she explained to me it was the tool she used to clean the toilet back home. Uggggh! But those were exciting days as we were making those adjustments and the first time that both of us had been away from our parents.

CHAPTER 12

MAN DOES NOT LIVE BY BREAD ALONE

I can honestly say that money has never motivated my ministry. As someone has said, "I don't preach to live but I do live to preach." When a love offering is placed in my hands at the end of a meeting I feel like a professional golfer or tournament bass fisherman who gets paid for what he loves to do. Confession must be made that there have been a very few times when churches, pastors or deacons have been less than honest and kept back part of the funds that people have given in good faith and yet part of that money went back into the church treasury. This is not just speculation, because pastors or church treasurers have told me of conferences being held at the close of a meeting and the decision being made that the offering was just too large to give to the visiting preacher. On those few occasions I must admit to anger and resentment.

Having stated the aforementioned, everyone understands that money is a necessity for survival. I have yet to have the ravens deliver food to my little brook and though I have carefully searched the mouths of several thousand fish I have yet to find one single coin for taxes or T-bones. It had long been a conviction of Carolyn's and mine that when children came into the home the woman was to be a keeper at home and that there was no higher calling given to womanhood than to nurture those children in the admonition of the Lord. As I have unflinchingly preached this from pulpits across America I have been castigated, rebuked and reviled by more than a few. We have been rewarded by seeing three sons grow into maturity as honest young men and two of them now are serving successful, God blessed pastorates. I have no problem with those who will genuinely disagree with this conviction, but what can take the place of a mother seeing a child take his or her first step or hearing the first words fall from those precious lips? It is a blessing too sweet and cherished to be shared with a day care teacher or even a grandparent.

A DIVINE INTERVENTION

Funds were running dangerously low and only one or two meetings had been scheduled that would provide some relief from pressing needs. The pastor of my home church had scheduled me for a revival in the late fall and we looked to that week with anticipation. I was hesitant to seek part time employment after classes because I was convinced the Lord was going to open doors for other revivals. The week before the Saturday for me to return to Birmingham for the meeting at the Sixty-Sixth Street Baptist Church, I developed strep throat. Fever was dangerously high and my throat was so sore I could hardly drink water without real discomfort. Eating food was out of the question. The Seminary Physician warned and advised me to stay in bed and cancel or reschedule the meeting. Perhaps unwisely his counsel was rejected.

Saturday morning came and the fever and discomfort still persisted, but in spite of all, I told Carolyn to call our friend, Jerry Smith, to come and drive me to the airport. She graciously packed the suitcase, pressed my dress shirts and placed my suits and sport coats in a hang up bag. Jerry came and loaded the bags and helped me into his car and with head hanging low we made our way to the airport. Finally I was onboard and into the air. In a few moments a kind stewardess came down the aisle with complimentary box lunches. Stopping at my seat she handed me one, but I declined due to the intense throat pain. As she walked away I felt impressed to call her back to my aisle seat and told her I had changed my mind. With throat discomfort still present, I carefully opened the plastic container, took a bite of the ham sandwich and was amazed to swallow with ease. The discomfort immediately vanished, the fever left and I realized the Great Physician had blessed His child. Without a doubt God had heard the prayers of Carolyn and me and the seminary friends that had been calling out to our Lord for His healing.

The eight-day revival was blessed of God. Some of my old high school buddies made lifelong commitments to the Lord. The building was packed for almost every service and more than thirty people confessed Jesus as Savior and Lord. My kind and gracious pastor, Harold Procter, did a masterful job in encouraging his people to participate in a love offering each service and we were presented with largest gift we had ever received.

There would be many more times when our faith would be challenged and stretched, but never without Him proving Himself faithful or without His comfort whereby we would be able to comfort others with the same comfort whereby we had been comforted.

The revival at 66th Street Baptist following God's healing.

ABSENTEE STUDENT

Back at school the next week, attending classes, we began a routine that would prove to be a blessing and a burden. One of the reasons we were impressed to attend Southwestern Baptist Theological Seminary was because it had the reputation for being the most conservative theologically and also the most evangelistic. Almost without exception my professors were very supportive of my call into evangelism and permitted me to be away from campus as much as one week out of every month. Friends were permitted to make carbon copies of class notes, take tape recorders when possible and occasionally Carolyn would attend and take shorthand. I mention that it was a burden in that it was tremendously difficult to keep up and make good grades. I soon learned that Greek was an impossibility to be absorbed without daily attendance in class. As other doors continued to open I found myself driving as much as 200 miles after class to preach and would drag home at three o'clock in the morning for a brief nap and then back to class. Ah! But when you are young you are invincible, you think, and besides that you are convinced you are surely indispensable to the Kingdom. In future day's circumstances would remind me of my poor humanity and the frailty of the flesh.

CHAPTER 13

ON OTHER'S SHOULDERS

Any preacher, with enough sense to tie his shoes, realizes that any so called success in his ministry is because he is privileged to stand on the shoulders of others. Every man of God would do well to write his own last chapter of Romans where we find Paul listing and identifying those to whom he owed a debt of gratitude for aiding him in his ministry. Later I will include such a sacred list, but just now I must mention a tremendous old saint of God who was to launch and sustain my personal service as an evangelist.

CASSIUS ELIJAH AUTREY

If ever one tried to visualize the Old Testament Elijah challenging the false prophets of Baal, he would only have to see Dr. C.E. Autrey turned loose in evangelism class or standing behind the pulpit with the anointing of God upon him. With a Scofield Bible in one hand and his fist lifted above his head with outstretched arm and perspiration on his brow, he was a blessing to behold and hear. Some days he would say, "Close those doors to the hallway, I am just going to preach to you today."

And I have more than once left that classroom with such a burning in my heart that I would drive to downtown Ft. Worth and share the Gospel on the street corners. He had little use for shy compromising preachers and one day in his excited exhortation rebuked us not having courage saying, "Some fellows are afraid they are going to upset some old constipated woman."

On another occasion he stated he carried that Scofield Bible under his arm just to irk some of the too straight-laced professors. He was used of the Lord to "set a fellow's shucks on fire" as he would describe it.

My personal great debt of gratitude is because of the exposure he gave me to his classes. Each new semester he would invite me into each of his classes, encouraging me to wear a coat and tie that day, and he would introduce me to all the students, complementing me far beyond my ability. Because of that kindness many, many doors of opportunity were opened not only during those seminary days, but also in the years to come as friendships were bonded and young pastors went to churches all over the country.

BROTHER MAC

Another God send was a kind and gracious professor of music, Edwin Mcneely, better known as Brother Mac. He had never received an earned doctorate and because of his unconventional and maverick style and personality, he was not on the Hit Parade among many of the other faculty and especially in the Music Department that tended to be on the highbrow side. Every ministerial student had to take one semester of music appreciation and since most of us didn't know a sharp from a flat nor an octave from a contralto it was a mad rush each new semester to get in Mac's class to be assured of passing. He had a heart for less than musically inclined preachers, but he shared homespun philosophy that was priceless.

Not many months after enrolling as a student, I was asked to conduct a revival at the old Calvary Baptist Church close to downtown Ft. Worth and I was there introduced to Mac as the music evangelist for the week. Though the church was located in a declining area and morale was waning, God saw fit to come down in power and there were real evidences of revival and a number of people were saved.

From that time on our relationship grew and we were in many meetings together and he also recommended me to his students and gave glowing and probably exaggerated reports to his friends on the faculty.

Mac had led the music many years before for an old Texas cowboy evangelist named B.B. Crimm who had a reputation of taking on and whipping tough old sinners that would mock him or his message. Mac had been friends with B.B. McKinney, author of many of our old hymns and was friends with Billy Sunday and his music evangelist. I reveled in the stories he would share with me in our days together. That cherished friendship lasted past his retirement and until his home going to be with Jesus years later.

Mac and I were in a meeting in a church in Arlington, Texas. Things got off to a slow start and went downhill from there. In those early days I labored under the unrealistic delusion that revival was going to come in every church. Situations like that burdened my heart beyond description and most often I felt personally responsible for the failure. One night in this particular church he joined me in prayer just before the service. After the closing amen of our time of fervent intercession Mac looked at me and asked, "Bobby, do you know what is wrong in this church and why revival hasn't come?"

"No, I don't, but if you know please tell me." With total seriousness and solemn expression of face he said, "These folks just don't give a damn."

Seeing my shock at his abrupt and unusual choice of words he continued, "Now Bobby, I mean a Tinker's dam."

I must confess that I was disappointed with his description until later turning to Webster's dictionary and discovering the definition of "Tinker's dam" is 'worthless, of no use." First time ever I concurred with what I thought was a swear word.

One day in class, Bro. Mac sought to give the preacher boys some much needed advice about platform decorum. He said, "Now fellows, it's alright to pull out your handkerchief and blow your nose, but for God's sake, you don't have to look at it!"

CHAPTER 14

HE PROVES HIMSELF FAITHFUL

The many opportunities to share the Word during those days at Southwestern made it possible to rely on the honorariums and love offerings for the material needs of life, and most appreciated was the fact that Carolyn was able to still be a stay at home mom. I was preaching during the school months and would return to Alabama for back-to-back meetings from June to August. Many of these meetings were in small country churches and sometimes the offerings would hardly cover expenses, but we could only bless the Lord for the privilege to be used by Him.

The first couple of years in seminary were the most difficult financially and yet we hardly realized it because many of our friends lived hand to mouth too. On one occasion when funds were all but depleted we went to A.L. Davis Grocery and bought three pounds of wieners for $1.00 and felt grateful that we could. We would open a can of Spam and stick clove buds in the top and bake it in the oven. On Friday nights several couples would come together and pool our food with laughter over the situation.

One of the bleakest occasions came when the cupboard was bare and the Joshua Baptist Church was asking me to consider coming to be their pastor. I had preached a revival there some months before and for whatever reason they were impressed enough to extend the invitation. The steady weekly income and the more than adequate parsonage presented a real temptation and yet I felt strongly that I was to remain in evangelism. I can still vividly remember kneeling beside the bed with tears and telling the Lord of my willingness to be a pastor, but that if He wanted me to remain in the present ministry I needed a word, a sign, an evidence and it had to be in haste.

We never had Monday classes, but on Tuesday after chapel service I went by my mailbox, 22266, peered in the window and saw a letter. Opening the box and taking out the letter I noted the return address, Mr. Preston Hicks and gave a Houston address. The name meant nothing to me, but I did hold it up to the sunlight coming through the window to see if there just might be some currency inside and seeing none I simply placed it within the pages of one of my books and dashed to my next class, Pastoral Ministry. Now please don't repeat this, but that was the dullest class imaginable. We nicknamed the professor as, 'The Fire Marshall', because if you had any fire he could extinguish it in three minutes flat. This day was no exception and as the good Doctor droned on and on and massive boredom surrounded me like a fog, suddenly I remembered the letter in my briefcase. Thinking to myself that a letter from an unknown person surely offered more stimulation than this, I quietly opened the envelope. The letter began by saying that though we had never met he had visited in a revival I had preached at the Broadway Baptist Temple some months before. He went on to say that he had come into an insurance settlement and felt impressed that he should send the enclosed check after obtaining my address from the church secretary. And there it was, a cashier's check for $125.00! That might not seem like much today, but I will tell you that in the late fifties it was humongous, and my friend, the fire fell in Pastoral Ministry that day.

Seeing the postmark on the envelope exactly matching the day of my earnest intercession for God to intervene provided a lasting, lifetime word from Him that said, "Son, don't worry about finances, no one else needs to know, just trust Me and seek first The Kingdom and these things will be added unto you." These were difficult, but delightful days indeed.

MOVING TO A NEW HOME

I must share another blessing from our lovely Lord that was graciously bestowed upon us during those refining seminary days. We had not spent many months renting the little duplex on West Waggoman when I was introduced to a fine, soul winning Christian laymen, Monte O'Neil, who was in the construction business. He had a home in Ft. Worth and in Birmingham, spending time in both locations. I had known him through reputation for he had been instrumental in leading my very best friend, Daryl Jones, to Jesus about four years earlier. In conversation with Monte and his son it was mentioned that he had a small house on West Spurgeon Street that was vacant, three blocks from the campus, and needed an occupant.

The O'Neils built and sold Jim Walter type shell homes and we were told that this particular house was nearly finished but the buyer had suddenly left town and abandoned the place. After legal procedures were followed we took possession of the spacious 500 sq. ft. dwelling for $3,750 with monthly payments of $47.50. Fortunately, I had worked for a contractor after high school graduation and with the help of friends, my brother, and after scavenging items, we completed the little mansion, installing a floor furnace, putting tile on the bathroom and kitchen walls, painting rooms with any paint available, one bedroom bright orange and another pink. Poorly insulated, the curtains stood at attention when the 'blue northers' blew in. I grant you that we would never have won a Better Homes and Gardens award, but we were one of the very few seminary couples who could boast of having their very own home.

That little abode still fills our minds with fond memories. It was before disposable diapers and the ability to afford an automatic dryer. We would wash the clothes in an old fashion washing machine that had rollers to squeeze out the wash water. (For you young folks, I suggest you venture to some museum to understand the contraption). Having dried the clothes to a soggy dampness, they were hung on clotheslines in the back yard. The hot dry Texas wind, with the temperature in the 100-degree plus range, would dry the garments before you could reach the end of line. In the blasting winter blustery weather, with temperatures ten degrees below freezing, the clothes and diapers would come off the line frozen solid. One had to be careful not to break your underwear in two and you could stand your long johns up in a corner. Just a little Texas exaggeration, but not too much.

Tarantulas, horny toads, dust storms that blew dust though every crack and crevice of the house. Ah, but they were great days and we felt blessed of God to have our own little dwelling. The mortgage payments were $47.50 each month and quite often we were only able to pay the interest on the note, but it was ours and the Rockefellers could not have been more content.

CHAPTER 15

SURPRISE, ANOTHER BOY

The summer of 1961 was one of unusual expectation. We had discovered early in the year that we were to be parents again in late July and graduation was finally to come in January after squeezing a three-year course of study into four years. It certainly was not prudent to return to Alabama for the summer, as usual, so I commuted to meetings, but making sure that I had set aside three weeks in order to be with Carolyn when this baby was born. I was determined to not be an absentee father again, but ah, the best laid plans of men. Carolyn's mom and dad came to stay with us as the delivery due date approached, but again no bundle of joy, no sweet Melanie Ann, for we knew this just had to be a girl.

Finally, scheduled meetings were upon us and with the urging and encouragement of Carolyn and her mom, I unwisely headed east for engagements in Louisiana and Alabama.

On August 4th, that call came and I left the revival at Walnut Park Baptist in Gadsden, rushed to catch a flight to Ft. Worth and finally arrived at All Saints Hospital. Pushing Carolyn in a wheelchair, we made our way to the nursery window to get my first glimpse of our second born. Now I am not going to say the newborn was not pretty, but he was certainly no Melanie Ann! How that little tyke was to be later voted the most handsome in his graduation class is a compliment to the creative activity of God. But to this day I must confess, without prejudice of course, that Steven (Steve) Andrew Britt is one sharp looking young man and an outstanding teacher/preacher of God's Word.

Returning to Alabama the next day to close the meeting, I could hardly wait to be back with Carolyn and our two sons, to enroll for the fall semester and make plans for graduation in January. School days will soon be over and I am more than ready to get on with God's calling for my life and save the world.

September, our little family is back together again, a busy fall preaching schedule awaits and just five months to endure classes and that long cherished degree will be placed in my hand certifying that I am now a full-fledged, ordained, educated, flaming evangelist ready to be unleashed on an unsuspecting world!

On that night of graduation, I turned to one of my best friends, Ron Dunn, and sarcastically stated that it would be just my luck to have that certificate placed in my hand and suddenly Jesus would come back without the world having the opportunity to hear me preach! Little did I realize that the school of reality was about to be in session.

CHAPTER 16

BACK TO ALABAMA

Talk about prosperity, we were living proof. We had ventured off to seminary four years earlier with a four by eight U-Haul in tow and here we are returning to our beloved Birmingham pulling a five by twelve. With the equity from the sale our little mansion on West Spurgeon we were able to make a down payment on a beautiful, brand new three bedroom home in Center Point, a small but growing community just outside the city. Weary from the nonstop trek from Ft. Worth I made a worthless vow as we unloaded our possessions into that lovely house, "the next move I make will be to the funeral home." A vow made in haste is a vow made in waste.

Our dwelling on Hiawatha Drive became home base for the newly formed Bobby Britt Evangelistic Association. As I have stated before, I can honestly say that I have never preached with money as a motivation, but adequate finances are a necessity even for a preacher. December and January were always slack months on my calendar and one had to make 'make hay while the sun shined' so to speak. How else could we make the huge $98.00 a month house payment? To make ends meet it was necessary to book some meetings back to back and thus be away from home, sometimes as many as three weeks in a row.

It is impossible to express the homesickness, the loneliness and the sense of guilt in being away from your wife and children during those times. Though I missed Carolyn as much as I did the boys, I knew that she could understand the days and weeks of separation, but I grieved over Danny and Steve in the early days of their life.

THE FIRST OF MANY TESTINGS

It was the summer of 1962 and I was in revival at Dalraida Baptist Church in Montgomery, Alabama. I awoke one morning in the hotel and noticed a curtain of darkness in my left eye. John Smith, the pastor, made me an appointment with an ophthalmologist that day and he said it was a retinal detachment and suggested that I could preach, but without undue effort. That, of course, is all but impossible for me, and I preached the remaining days of the meeting and God greatly blessed with many coming to know Jesus as Savior. I realize now that my decision was quite foolish, but again when you are young, one feels indestructible and irreplaceable.

Returning to Birmingham on the following Monday, the diagnosis was confirmed and I was admitted to Caraway Hospital and remained there for a week with numbers of exams and seen by a host of physicians. Those were some of the pioneer days of retina surgery and it was finally determined that I should fly to New York to be treated by one of the foremost retina surgeons in America.

Now, dismissed from the hospital and returning home, plans were in order to fly to New York and be admitted to The Institute of Ophthalmology in the New York Presbyterian Hospital. There was a great deal of anxiety in the preparations. First, the cost was far beyond our means. What would we do with our boys? Where would Carolyn stay while we were there? And there were a dozen other considerations. There was the concern about her ability to journey with me and meet the demands of leading a husband, whose eyes were now both covered, through the airport terminals and finding transportation from Grand Central Station to the hospital. It was really more responsibility than a young lady in her early twenties should have to encounter, but she did an outstanding job, though she did lead me into one doorframe that nearly cracked my skull.

Finally, fatigued and apprehensive we made it to the facility and were admitted. Shortly, we were introduced to Dr. Graham Clark, the head of the department of ophthalmology. He was so gracious and we found out later he had performed retina surgery on Arthur Godfrey, famous radio personality, and Bishop Sheen of the Catholic Church. Explaining that we had very inadequate insurance coverage he replied that there would be no fee as to his services, but only the hospital charges. After several more days of examination, surgery was scheduled and the procedure was performed. It would be several days before a prognosis would be delivered.

The next three weeks were followed by days of uncertainty and restlessness. Again, this was a time when retina surgery was in its formative days. My head was positioned between retainers on each side to make sure there was no movement and I was not permitted to stand or walk for a number of days.

I was placed in a four-bed ward with a Catholic, Sal DePompeo, a Jew, Emil Nitiche, and a young Episcopalian boy who was a skeptic, Jeff Dikett. It was a wonderful opportunity to witness for our Lord. Carolyn had been invited to stay with a cousin who lived in New Jersey in a gated community and had to travel over an hour a day to and from the hospital, but she never missed a day in visitation. When she was not there to feed me, I had to learn where the food was on the plate by the clock face method, potatoes at one o'clock, meat at three, etc.

Finally, after more than two weeks, Carolyn had to return home to care for the boys. I was released some days later, and with some fair amount of difficulty, flew back to Birmingham, still wearing pin holes, that were glasses that had shades on each side and small holes to see through in order to keep my eyes as immobile as possible. During the flight home I looked at the release forms and came to the page that read, 'prognosis, very grave'. My heart sank.

There has never been a more exciting homecoming than when the DC 7 landed in Birmingham and I was able to take Carolyn in my arms and kneel down to kiss and hug Steve and Danny.

Within a matter of weeks I was back on the road again, preaching His Word, seeing revival and souls come to Jesus. As long as I could do that, being a one-eyed, cross-eyed preacher was no big deal. It was to take us a number of years to pay off the hospital bill, but little by little, the debt was settled, made a bit difficult realizing the surgery had not succeeded.

TRAGEDY BRINGS A DECISION

It was in the mid sixties when I received a phone call from a fellow evangelist informing me of the death of the son of one of our mutual friends who was also a comrade in evangelism. The teen-age son had taken his life by hanging himself in their backyard. The father of the young man was away from home preaching meetings as much as eight weeks at a time and had expressed to me to his regret and his intention to cut back because he knew it was taking a toll on his family. That very day I put Danny in the car with me, drove some blocks away from our home, pulled the car off the road and promised him I would never be away again for more than eight days at a time except on very rare occasions. It was a vow I was able to keep and one that our Lord richly rewarded.

OUR THREE SONS

The Mod Squad in the early Seventies.
Carolyn, Barry, Steve, Me, and Danny.
Dig those leisure suits!

It was 1966 and we knew that Carolyn was near the end of her third pregnancy. All of our children were planned and gladly welcomed and received. We loved our two sons and were looking for a girl this third time. We had chosen the name of Melanie Ann for this third bundle of joy. I was determined to be available for this birth and scheduled meetings only in the Birmingham area. I was preaching a revival at Glenn Memorial Baptist in Bessemer, less than forty- five minutes from home. One night during the time of invitation, I could hear the ringing of the telephone in the pastor's office. I knew it was someone calling to inform me that Carolyn was on the way to the hospital. Closing the invitation, I called home and my instinct was confirmed. I arrived at the hospital shortly after Carolyn and sat by her bedside though most of the night and early morning hours. Being advised that the birth was some hours away, I returned home for a couple of hours sleep and then made way back to the birthing ward. A couple of hours latter Carolyn brought forth our third son, Barry Lunceford Britt. Again, no little girl, but we could not have experienced any greater joy, and in the succeeding years that bliss has only intensified.

I was strictly informed that there would be no Melanie Ann and finally when our middle son, Steve, and his wife Tana, had the thrill of having two daughters, they were the first females born into the Britt family in more than sixty-five years, and I must admit that there is something special about little girls.

SOME RELFCTIONS OF REGRET

In reflection of those twenty consecutive years of evangelism the most difficult aspect was that of separation from the family. More than once I can vividly remember tears welling up in my eyes as the airplane would taxi down the runway to fly from Birmingham on Saturday afternoon for the next meeting. Few hours are more lonesome than returning to a motel room totally fatigued from preaching your heart out, almost too weary to undress for the night. Difficult not only for me, but also for the family the Lord had graciously given to me. Carolyn had to get the boys off to school by herself, nurse them through the mumps and measles, sit in church alone, and often when couples would gather at a restaurant after church on Sunday night she felt like a fifth wheel.

Some time ago, I was rummaging through our garage and came upon a number of date books, held together by a rotting rubber band. I took the books that were records of meetings I had preacher over the years. Sitting on the edge of the bed and opening those small volumes, remembering the weeks of the blessings of God, I broke down and heavily sobbed. It was not a pity party, but in that time of reflection, I wept as I contemplated the many days, months and years when I had been absent for some of the best days in the lives of our sons. How many ball games missed, school plays when other dads were present, experiences never to be repeated. As I wept, I wondered, would I be willing to do it again?

REJOICE WITH THOSE THAT REJOICE?

I will always remember one occasion especially. I was in a Texas border town preaching in a large prestigious Baptist Church. The churches of the city had been engaged in a citywide crusade at the local stadium. A well-known preacher had led in the services and now local churches were following up with meetings hoping to encourage the new converts to become involved and identify with the congregations. The closing service had just concluded in the stadium and the pastor with whom I was serving and several others and I were invited to attend a fellowship meal in the home of a very wealthy, multimillionaire layman, he was known as, 'The Onion King of the USA.' In the group was a lovely TV personality who had her own weekly nationwide production. I confess to more than a degree of pride and felt that I had finally arrived. I was so impressed with where I was preaching, where I was dining and with whom I was associating. My host insisted that I call my wife and of course charge it to his residence. With excitement I called Carolyn and informed her about the services of the day, telling her of the people who were saved and then describing the elegance of the palatial home I was enjoying, the sumptuous food that was served and the guests with whom I was rubbing shoulders. Expecting to hear her express how proud she was of me I was surprised by the long pause and then shocked as I heard her break into sobs on the other end of the line. With some disgust she told me how she had just sat down to a hotdog and the difficulty she had in getting the boys to bed. I learned afresh that it is fairly easy to weep with those that weep, but often difficult to rejoice with those that rejoice. Whatever reward, if any, I receive at His coming, it will not compare with that given to the gallant wife who never expressed any fear of being home alone at night and never voiced dissatisfaction with God's call upon her life, the wife of a traveling evangelist.

Those college and seminary days and the fifteen years that followed still bring sweet reflection, blessings beyond my fondest dreams and certainly privileges and grace surpassing merit or deserving. Yes, there were times of pain and sorrow, separation and some sacrifice, disappointments and discouragements, but the positive so much surpasses the negative that the former are hardly remembered and those less than the best proved to be the most helpful in my much needed spiritual development.

In pages to follow we will return to examine some of those experiences.

A SPEECHLESS PREACHER

It was mid-summer of 1973 and I was thirty-seven years old. I was preaching a meeting in Decatur, Ala. On Friday night I returned to Birmingham to spend the night and take Carolyn and the boys back to the revival with me to enjoy the luxury motel where I was lodging and to enjoy the Olympic swimming pool. In the wee morning hours I awoke with a rushing sound of wind in my left ear and with horrific vertigo. I realized that something, very out of the ordinary, was happening and I reached over and took Carolyn by the arm and said, "Honey, I am dying." As she turned on the light I was suddenly and totally paralyzed on the entire left side of my body. As she began to question me, I became terrified when I realized I could not say or utter one single word. In moments the fear subsided and a peace filled my soul, and I became convinced I was about to go be with the Lord. Unable to communicate with Carolyn, all I knew to do was to smile and try to convey to her that all was well and for her to not panic. She later told me how stupid I looked with one side of my mouth turned upward and the paralyzed side of my mouth pulled and drawn down. An ambulance was called and as we sped toward East End Hospital, fear gripped my entire being as I realized I had suffered a stroke and the thought of lifelong paralysis and the inability to speak brought terror to my soul. The contemplation of being unable to preach was more then I could bear.

In the emergency room, doctors and nurses scurried about and as I lay on the table I was silently crying out to God. Suddenly, I heard my voice pierce the room, "Jesus!" Only one word, but oh, the blessedness of that cry. Until this day, I never hear that song, "There Is Just Something About That Name", that that experience does not flood my mind and soul.

In a matter of hours feeling and movement began to occur and the paralysis slowly faded away, and speech, though slurred, was returning. In nine days I was out of he hospital and only two meetings were canceled, and then on the road again. God is good, all the time.

A FREEING DISCOVERY

From the earliest days of my ministry, I was aware that I was somewhat of an odd duck. I say that not as a compliment or a complaint. Some friends and foes told me I was too hard as a preacher. One of my dearest pastor friends, one who invited me for several revivals, jokingly nicknamed me Boanerges. Perhaps you remember those were the names given to the brothers, James and John, by Jesus. It meant 'Sons of Thunder." I honestly struggled with the strong tendency to be, what appeared, abrasive in my preaching. I analyzed myself and was psychoanalyzed by others. On two occasions, during the racial struggles of the sixties, my life was threatened because I dared to say that forced segregation that excluded any person from attending God's church was wrong.

Often, as I sat on the platform waiting the time to preach, I struggled with God concerning those things I felt He had laid on my heart to share. Many times the words of Isaiah came to mind or I would turn to those verses and scan them and a sense of peace and courage would come to my heart:

> *Isaiah 58:1*
> *"Cry aloud, spare not, lift up thy voice like a trumpet, and shew my people their transgression, and the house of Jacob their sins."*

And still needing reassurance, I would turn to the prophet Ezekiel and read:

> *Ezekiel 3:8-9*
> *"Behold, I have made thy face strong against their faces, and thy forehead strong against their foreheads.*
> *"As an adamant harder than flint have I made thy forehead: fear them not, neither be dismayed at their looks, though they be a rebellious house."*

Surely, this type preaching closed many doors of opportunity, but more doors were opened than shut. Many, many complimented this type ministry and announced that they were thrilled that their children heard things they had never heard before. They attributed courage to me, but I explained, I feared to *not say* what God had placed on my heart. My fear of Him far outweighed any fear I had of man.

Some years later, I attended a conference led by a fellow named Bill Gothard. In that meeting a great deal of time was spent studying Spiritual Gifts. As the characteristics of the gift of prophecy were delineated, for the first time, I realized, 'Hey, that's me.' I understood that this was not some personality quirk or spiritual maladjustment, but this was the motivational gift God had placed in my life. That discovery has not relieved all the spiritual tension in my ministry. I still tussle with the desire to be more tender in my preaching, but I have become comfortable with the criticism that comes with the exercising of that gift.

One needs to understand that the gift of prophecy is not identified as one who tells or forecasts the future, but rather, it is one who simply speaks forth the Word of God. The prophet does not see things in different shades of gray, but in his concept it is either right or wrong, black or white.

I hasten to say that one who has the gift of a prophet has no excuse for being rude or unkind and anytime that gift is void of a broken heart, the prophet is abusing the spiritual endowment bestowed upon his life. I must add that this is the gift most needed in the church today and it is with sadness I conclude, it is the least appreciated. Too many pastors and people don't want to be spiritually disturbed.

CHAPTER 17

CHARTING THROUGH NEW WATERS

I am convinced that God never changes His will for a person's life, but He does often change one's direction in life. An example is the Apostle Paul. We see him as the writer of the epistles, an evangelist, a missionary, a pastor and a prisoner. I would in nowise compare my ministry to his, but I must confess his varied opportunities afforded real encouragement to my heart in days to come.

About the year of 1975 I began to experience strange disturbances in my heart. The Lord continued to fill my calendar with opportunities for evangelistic ministry, but these new stirrings troubled me. Vividly, I recall mentioning to Carolyn one morning that I felt that the Lord was going to do a new thing in our lives. Another day we drove past a church where I had preached three revival meetings and commented that if I should ever pastor a church, I would like for it to be one like that particular fellowship. The oddity of that statement was that though I had several opportunities to be pastor, not once had I sensed this was God's will for my life.

Not long afterward, we were informed by Carolyn's physician that she needed a fairly serious surgery. He was aware of some emotional scars caused by my absence for the birth of two of our three sons so he strongly advised me to clear my calendar in order to be by her side during the period of recovery. It was during this time that I received a call from the aforementioned church asking if I could fill their pulpit for the very same six weeks.

During those weeks the Lord graciously blessed with great liberty in sharing the Word and a number of decisions for

Christ were made. Lord's Day-by-Lord's Day people would graciously compliment the messages and tell me that I should consider being their pastor. Brushing aside their comments I would inform them that in a brief time they would soon grow weary of me, and yet deep in my heart, I was becoming keenly aware that this was His Will for my life. The prospect frightened me out of my wits. I knew that I did not have the pastor's heart and the task of preparing three new messages a week was a responsibility far beyond my capability.

As I sought His face in those days, not only did He burden my heart to accept the challenge, I began to fear that the Pastor Search Committee might not even ask me to consider the opportunity.

In due time a meeting was held with the committee and they grilled me and I grilled them. I shared with them my philosophy of ministry based on my understanding of the Word. Experientially, I knew little about how to pastor a God blessed church, but I had been in hundreds of churches through those twenty years of evangelism and had observed what the Lord honored and what brought genuine, sustained growth to a fellowship. They affirmed their agreement and within a week I was called to be the Pastor of Hilldale Baptist Church located just outside Birmingham in the rapidly growing area of Center Point. It was February of 1977, a new beginning and a new chapter in our lives.

Though my know-how of being the pastor was severely limited, I was convinced that what God blessed was week-by-week Bible exposition. I had seen a small congregation explode almost overnight under the ministry of a charismatic, dynamic young man who led the people in program after program. It reminded me of a Wrestle Mania mentality that demanded the church do something this week more spectacular than last week. It was not long before a new auditorium had to be built to accommodate the crowds. The church and the young preacher were the talk of the town and the state convention. The tragedy was that not many months later, the sharp motivator resigned, and in a few months the numbers dwindled, and the few remaining were strapped with tremendous building debt.

Here is another impressive observation, a sharp contrast. I had preached two meetings where the pastor remained for nearly forty years. He was anything but dynamic, low key, not a snappy dresser, but a man who spent long hours in his study and fed his people the Word every time the doors were opened. The second revival I preached found the attendance larger and the church healthier. When he resigned there was no drop in attendance and the fellowship continued in growth.

The contrast, along with other such experiences, made an indelible impression on my life and left me with strong conviction that the Biblical will for the pastor, the man of God, was to bury yourself in the Book, have a Word from the Lord every time the people come together and thereby "equip the saints to do the work of the ministry."

To any young preacher who might read these words, I would offer a word of caution. If he should dare to do this there is a price to pay. Though I had shared this conviction with the Pastor Search Committee as well as with the people from the pulpit, there were those who constantly complained, "Our pastor is not available." And sure enough, I wasn't. Each morning I would come to the office and then venture to a small five by eight foot room, hidden away on the third floor to dig into the Word and seek His face until noon. If a phone call came my secretary was instructed to tell the caller that I was not in the office (which was true) but that I could be reached in case of an emergency.

It was unbelievable how the Lord blessed this new discipline. I had been so concerned that there would not be enough to say on Wednesday nights and twice on Sunday and suddenly I was frustrated that there was too much to say. For seven years most of our people came to the services with anticipation of a Word from the Lord. It was a blessing beyond description to hear the rustling of the pages of the Bible when the pastor asked the people to open the Book and to see young and old alike taking notes. And how our gracious God blessed! Attendance almost doubled, the mid-week service went from thirty or forty meeting in the fellowship hall to two hundred as we moved to the auditorium. Before too long the balcony was filled Sunday by Sunday and a large number of people came to know Jesus as Lord and Savior. Families were reunited, drunks were converted, young people were called into the ministry, buildings were built and renovated, and all in all, it seemed that heaven came down and glory filled our souls. During the seven years I was privileged to pastor the church we baptized over 550 people.

DARK DAYS OF CONFLICT

As might be expected, all was not halleluiah and everyone was not shouting glory. The complaint of the pastor not always being available was murmured often. (Someone has said that if one is always available he is not worth much when he is. And I concur.) I remain convinced that a shepherd can minister to two dozen people a week by constantly being in the homes and always in his office or he can get alone with God and stand and preach and minister to over a hundred or twice that many each week, but sad to say many folks had rather have a handshaking, back slapping, coffee drinking preacher. Undeterred, I kept the same schedule.

As often is the case, when a church does grow rapidly, new leadership begins to emerge and those who have been in places of some authority feel threatened. Perhaps I was too idealistic, but the standard was held high and as it was shared from the pulpit that teachers and deacons and all persons in places of leadership should be faithful to all the services of the fellowship and engaged in visitation and soul winning. Most of the people, and especially those who had come into the church in the first five years of my ministry there, were in agreement. As new teachers were selected, deacons ordained and committees appointed, some of the old guard was replaced, but not without voices of discontent.

I am acutely aware that it is difficult, if not impossible, to be totally objective when one is involved in church dissent, but as best one can know his heart, my desire was for the Lord to be glorified in His Church. Certainly mistakes were made on my behalf, but my motives were pure.

Opposition became organized and some dissenters held small clandestine meetings and orchestrated methods to hold the pastor in check. One fellow, of some wealth and influence, and his wife came to my office to notify me that they felt it was time for me to resign, and that he had enough sway to get the job done. My answer was that if he could do that he should be about the task, but if God wanted me to stay his efforts would be in vain.

Church conferences often became bitter. Harsh words were hurled, insults and injuries became common. Though the dissenters were in the minority, God's Holy Spirit was grieved and ministry became more and more difficult. It disturbed me that many of the young believers were confused and hurt and discouraged. For months I asked the Lord to let me resign and be released from the burden of responsibility, but over and over He seemed to say, "Stay."

A few obscene phone calls were directed to my wife, an accusation later came that I was complicit in a financial scam relating to a parking lot addition, and it was taking a toll on our sons.

One Saturday night a young man asked me to meet him in my office to discuss a problem that could not wait. As I walked into the office about two dozen men met me. They were disturbed about the rift in the church and suggested to me that I should resign and form a new fellowship with their families. They informed me that a large number of individuals had asked them to come to me with their request. I wept as I listened to their concern for me, and the assurance of their support. Again, I declined their suggestion, telling them that God had not allowed me to resign.

Finally, in February of 1984, during a difficult business meeting, I felt as though the Lord finally said it was time to go. As Carolyn and I walked out of that meeting I told her that God had released me. As I lay in the bed that night, I experienced such joy beyond description. It is without exaggeration that I felt as though I wanted to run up and down the hall of the parsonage, shouting, "Glory to God." The next morning as I drove to meet my buddy for a day of fishing, I did shout and sang praises to the Lord. A burden beyond description had been removed. The following Sunday I tendered my resignation. Yet, in all of this, I would be less than honest if I did not admit that in days and months to come I often second-guessed that decision.

CHAPTER 18

PLOWING NEW GROUND

Within a week after my resignation the associate pastor, the minister of music, the minister of youth, the pastor of counseling, and more than half the deacons resigned their positions along with the majority of Sunday School teachers. Approximately 200 people met at a local school the following Wednesday night and voted to ask me to become the pastor of a new church they intended to form. These were cream of the crop folks and I wept when I received the phone call that night informing me of their desire.

The next Sunday more than 200 dear people gathered at a nearby junior college and we had our first service. The request of some of the leadership was that we would be an independent Bible Church. I agreed that I could be their shepherd with the conditions that there would be no criticism of Southern Baptists and that I would be permitted to help form our doctrinal statement. Other than the plan to select elders and deacons, we differed not a whit from a Baptist fellowship.

One could not have asked nor prayed for a more desirable relationship with a group of believers. One of the first questions was how much I needed to meet our family needs. Yet, for some strange and yet to be understood reasons, the Lord would not let me know peace in this new place of service. For six months I struggled in prayer and often fasted about the situation. I felt that it would be treasonous to leave this new work. These people loved my family and me and humanly speaking they were where they were because of me. It was with severe agony that I stood and offered my resignation after little more than half a year. Some of my very best friends severely judged my motives and others voiced their disappointment with my decision.

Because we had made it known that we intended to become an independent Bible Church, many of my fellow Baptist friends wrote me off as some kind of a nut and doors were closed for any immediate hope of an opportunity for a return to evangelism. One scheduled meeting was cancelled as the pastor explained to me it, was his duty to 'protect his people,' therefore he could not take a chance on me coming and hurting his church. Admittedly, these were some of the darkest days of my life emotionally as I struggled to determine His will for my life.

CHAPTER 19

A GREAT DILEMMA

Forty-eight years old, suddenly no income, an uncertain future, held at arm's length by many of my preacher buddies, misunderstood by closet friends, these are elements that make for deep soul searching and the onslaught of depression. It was necessary to cash in insurance policies and withdraw what little money there was in a retirement program. For the first time since seminary days we were in financial stress. Slowly the Lord began to open the doors for revival and evangelism. My friend, Junior Hill, an evangelist who stayed booked for years in advance graciously recommended me for meetings he could not accept. Yet the days of booking twenty plus meetings and those of eight days in length were over. A sad transition was taking place. For a variety of reasons, or excuses, most local churches were not scheduling revivals as in days gone by. Where most fellowships had always had two or more meetings a year now most were having only one or none and most of those were four day meetings at the most. The next six years proved to be times of testing.

Gradually the doors of opportunity began to open as pastors began to realize that my convictions and doctrinal positions had not changed, but I became more aware of the changes evident in the local church. As previously mentioned many pastors no longer scheduled revival meetings and those that did planned only for Sunday through Wednesday. My heart had always been burdened for real revival in the church with the result of lost people coming to know Jesus as Savior. For years I had spent the first few services preaching to those who had been saved, but had grown cold in their walk with the Lord. As God would bring His people to repentance, revival would begin to break out in the church and I would begin preaching to the lost and many times would see a harvest of souls. It soon saddened my heart to see so few lost people now coming to the services and so few of God's people in attendance. I became convinced this was the reason so many pastors chose not to schedule an evangelist nor plan revival meetings. To many, they were reluctant to set aside days for revival when his own people would not attend.

This was a phenomenon I had not experienced in the previous twenty years of evangelism and I found myself preaching mainly to the people who had already professed to know Jesus as Savior and though some were still converted it was not like the old days when it was not unusual to see forty, fifty or more come to Christ in an eight day meeting. Many of my fellow evangelists left the ministry of itinerant evangelism as fewer and fewer churches issued a call for their services. I felt like a friend of mine who in jest referred to himself as a 'remnant preacher.' Though it was a rewarding ministry in that I saw God bless in the reviving of His people and some Christians claiming a deeper walk with the Lord, my heart yearned to see God's Spirit break the hearts of the lost and bring them with repentance and faith coming to Him. Admittedly it was a new and difficult adjustment.

Little did I realize that another valley was ahead.

BLINDSIDED

I had resigned my last pastorate in the late summer of 1985 and now was back into the ministry of evangelism for two years. Doors were still opening, but many meetings were in small churches and honorariums were often inadequate, but our needs were being met.

One morning I awoke and to my shock discovered that there was a black curtain blocking a quarter of my vision in my right eye. I immediately knew that the problem was a detached retina. I had lost my left eye to a detachment in 1963. In those earlier years retina surgery was almost in its infancy and I had spent a month in the Institute of Ophthalmology in New York. Although I had one of the best surgeons in the country, Dr. Graham Clark who had operated on Arthur Godfrey and Cardinal Spelman, the procedure was unsuccessful.

Now I was rattled with fear that blindness might possibly be my fate for the rest of my life and I must admit that the tears flowed freely that day as our middle son, Steve, drove me to the Eye Foundation in Birmingham. Dr. David Davidson, a friend in grade school, high school and college, was there to meet me. As he examined me as I lay flat on my back, he reminded me and my son how I chased him down and beat him up more than once on the school grounds, and I must admit a definite uneasiness as he talked about the surgery he was about to perform.

Bless the Lord that the operation was a success though I was left with some visual impairment and was now experiencing double vision to a degree. Study and driving became more difficult and in a few months a cataract began to rapidly develop. Discouragement and sporadic depression was a daily battleground. Foolishly I tempted the Lord by continuing to drive to meetings and often found myself in dangerous situations plus endangering the lives of others. Only the mercy of our Lord prevented me from disaster on several occasions.

Finally, I came to the place where I had to ask friends to drive me to preach. When I traveled by plane I would have to ask someone to read the monitors in the airport concourses.

The doctors would not perform cataract surgery because of fear of infection or hemorrhage that would leave me totally blind. Eventually, I came to the place where I was willing to take the risk rather than tolerate the worsening condition. Sure enough, when the bandages were removed, I could only see bloody dots before my eyes, the result of a hemorrhage from the operation. But as days passed, the tiny dots of blood subsided and the surgery proved to be successful. A lens implant returned my vision to better than 20/20. Again, bless the Lord, oh my soul.

CHAPTER 20

A FAITH STRETCHING EVENT

Many times I have stated that the believer's most valuable spiritual asset or commodity is faith, and *that faith* is bestowed on the believer at the point or instance of salvation. Does He not say in Hebrews 11:6 that faith is that which pleases Him?

"But without faith it is impossible to please him:
for he that cometh to God must believe that he is,
and that he is a rewarder of them that diligently seek him."

And Peter elevates and evaluates this royal commodity when he states:

7 That the trial of your faith, being much more precious than of gold that perisheth, though it be tried with fire, might be found unto praise and honour and glory at the appearing of Jesus Christ".

Note that it is faith which is tried by fire that will bring honor and glory at the appearing of our Lord. It is God who gives, by grace, the ability to repent and trust Jesus as Lord and Savior.

Ephesians 2:8-9
"for it is by grace you have been saved, through faith-and this not from yourselves, it is the gift of God not by works, so that no one can boast".

The entire process of salvation from beginning to end is His. He brings the conviction and He gives the longing, the desire to trust Him as Lord and Savior. He gives the grace that allows the sinner to believe and by faith to rest his full confidence in the finished work of Jesus, faith is that God given ability to reach out to embrace him as Savior. But, He never intends for that grace gift, that initial faith, to remain in its infancy. It is our Savior's objective for that faith to grow, to be ever increasing and the most effective process He uses to achieve His purpose is that of trial and testing. It is in the midst of those times that we are forced to throw ourselves on Him in totality. It is my opinion that our Lord allows difficulty to invade our lives in order to stretch our faith incrementally.

OBSERVING THE GROWING, THE PURIFYING, THE STRECHTING OF FAITH

In the Book of First Samuel, we read of David, the shepherd boy, killing Goliath the giant. But we should note that the faith that faced the challenge was not instantaneous. David himself shares those events that prepared him for confidence to kill the Philistine monster. He related how God had given him victory over a charging bear and a ferocious lion in previous days. If God could deliver those two beasts into his hands, surely that same Savior could and would defeat the feared blasphemer who stood before him mocking the God of Israel all the while. This is only one of the many examples of the Father incrementally growing, stretching and purifying the faith of one of his heroes in conflict.

I share the above conviction in order to relate one of the most faith stretching experiences of my life, an experience that was to prepare me for future valleys that were to be tread, valleys so dark and dismal that only a faith in God and His Word kept me going. I offer no apology for the rather lengthy composition in dealing with the following. It still stands as one of the most challenging experiences of my life and I pray will not prove to be too meticulous or boring as you relive it with me. It begins with:

A SUPRISING INVITATION

In 1986, I was elected to serve as President of the Alabama Conference of Southern Baptist Evangelists. I was privileged to begin that organization in the early sixties and this was my third time to serve as President. It was mainly a figurehead position with few real responsibilities, but this particular year it came with a special bonus.

Each president of each state, who had such fraternities, was invited by the Billy Graham Association to attend The World Congress on Evangelism, to be held in Amsterdam, as their guest. Airfare, hotel accommodations, all meals and materials were to be included. 1986 had not been a good year for me, too few meetings, financial strain, failing vision and intermittent battles with depression. The phone call from the Home Mission Board with this opportunity was a halleluiah tonic for my sad soul. As I walked down the stairs from my study, I stopped midway, sat down and wept out the good news to Carolyn. Little did I know that that invitation was going to bring about the most faith demanding, faith stretching, faith growing, and challenging experience of my entire life.

OFF TO AMSTERDAM

There was an electrifying excitement as the huge 747 lifted from the Atlanta runway and made its slow turn to the east. Aboard the flight were dozens of fellow evangelists, some I had never met, others known for decades but separated by circumstances, some whose ministries were heralded in mostly small fellowships and some who were the so called 'big shots' among the field of evangelists, but all sharing in a close knit, common comradery. As we shared our fellowship in the Lord, spoke of His abundant blessings on our ministries, like challenges we had all endured, the touchdown in the Netherlands seemed to be a short excursion indeed.

THE POOR RICH PEOPLE

More than 9,000 evangelists were in attendance from all over the world, with the majority coming from third world countries. Many, many were there whose abject poverty was evident. Some with threadbare suits, worn out shoes, some had never seen an escalator nor elevator. Most had only seen airplanes high overhead and now had flown to the conference. It was an overwhelming and humbling experience to say the least. Franklin Graham and Samaritans Purse did a phenomenal job in clothing, providing shoes and socks for these dear people.

During the week I spoke with and came to know fellow servants from Africa, South America, from many of the Asian countries, Korea, the Philippines and on and on. I was moved by their zeal for God. They related wonderful stories of people packing out auditoriums just to hear the gospel message in their poverty filled cities and many asked me for a business card or an address. When the last meeting had closed I was sitting in the airport with a number of friends from the states and a number of representatives of our Southern Baptist Foreign Mission Board. I shared with them my burden for those I had met and expressed my desire to go to be with them in evangelistic efforts. One of the heads of one of the departments spoke a word of caution urging me to not be too hasty in volunteering to accept an invitation from individuals in the various countries, but to work through our Mission Board. It was sound advice mingled with a bit of wisdom, but counsel I did not heed, much to my regret.

Some days after returning to Birmingham I received a letter from a pastor of several churches inviting me to come to his East African country to lead in a number of outdoor crusades. I responded by writing to him that I would make it of definite prayer. Two weeks later he wrote again thanking me for my *acceptance* of his invitation and included a flyer announcing my coming to conduct pastor schools and preach 'crusades,' Frantically, I began trying to reach him by telephone to correct his misunderstanding and explain I could not come on such short notice. I discovered that any phone service was most primitive and that there was absolutely no way to reach him. As I sought the face of God in the troublesome matter I sensed a definite impression that all of this was in the plan and will of the Lord and that I was to make the hurried plans to go.

Plans were put in order. Already, I had a passport, and when I called the Embassy of his country a visa was expedited. I was informed later that no visa had ever been issued with such haste. A number of friends heard of my dilemma and contributed financially. My home church, Roebuck Park Baptist, paid for the travel expenses. Calling the Health Department, I received information as to shots and immunizations that had to be given in sequence, and as only God can plan it, I received my *last shot on the very last day possible before I was to board the plane.*

WHO BUT GOD?

The very night before I was to fly out of Atlanta I received a phone call from a man introducing himself as Gene Covington, a Southern Baptist missionary on his way back to Ghana, the country of my destination. This again could only be the Providence of God, as he explained how he and his wife had stopped in Birmingham for a visit to the Jefferson Health Department to get their final shots for their return to Ghana and were informed by one of the nurses that another minister had been in the clinic earlier that day and that I was to leave the next morning for the same West African country. He contacted me to see if there was any questions he might be able to answer and what advice he might offer. When I informed him of my plans and schedule to be with only a local pastor, I heard a low groan. He then asked the cities where I was to lodge and preach and there was a long pause. As kindly and diplomatically as possible, he explained to me my need of caution. As he spoke to me of the desperate conditions of my destination city my heart began to sink. By the Providence of God he gave me a contact, a denominational hostel in the city of Accra, a facility where missionary kids resided and were tutored while their parents ministered in the interior. It was with uneasiness that I laid my head on my pillow that night of December 16, 1986 and moments of sleep were scarce in those hours of darkness.

Another confirmation that this trip, though ill advised by all appearances, was the will of the Father. I had wondered earlier how I would get to Atlanta for my departure. I was hesitant about driving to Atlanta and leaving my car in storage for two weeks. Three days before I was to leave a friend called informing me that he had heard of my need and that he was to drive a van to Atlanta the very day of my flight. He had volunteered to return some sound equipment that had been rented for Roebuck Park Baptist church used in a Christmas program. When he arrived to provide transportation to the airport, I led in prayer as Carolyn, Sam Cargo and I held hands. I wept as I was now so uneasy about this mission engagement.

There now came the realization that I had placed myself in a situation where I would lose all contact with my friends and family for two weeks. Communication would be all but impossible and no mission board would know how to be responsible for my safety. And yet, with all the apprehension there was a peace and an assurance that too many things had come together for this not to be the will of God for my life.

ANGEL UNAWARE?

On the final leg of the flight from Amsterdam to Accra, the capital city of Ghana, I was assigned a seat next to a man from Ireland, on his way to that city to service antiquated telephone equipment, another Divine appointment from our loving God. He informed me of some of the difficulties I would encounter upon landing. His concerns were not exaggerated. Once on the ground, the aircraft parked several hundred yards from the terminal for security reasons, because of political instability. I made my way into the terminal and stood in one of several lines for visa and passport examination. Making my way to retrieve my luggage I was met and examined by a suspicious customs agent who opened every solitary piece of the same. A mass of humanity pushed and shoved almost every step of the way. I became almost frantic as I stood near the exits looking for someone who would recognize me as the guest preacher, for I certainly had not a clue as to who was to meet me.

After about a half hour I realized I was in a country where I knew not one person, where American currency could not be exchanged and there was no one to call and nowhere to lay my head for the night. It appeared that my only option was to re-board the KLM 747 and head back home with my tail tucked between my legs. Ah, but again our Lord was to show Himself strong and faithful!

Fortunately, the friend from Ireland had not yet left the airport and seeing my dilemma he invited me to ride with him in the taxi sent for him. As we walked through the exit to the parking area I was again astounded by the scene before me. Dozens of men waited outside hoping to carry luggage or provide transportation to arriving passengers and they pushed and shoved each other violently and even struck one another to determine who would be hired, paid or tipped. It was just the beginning of the culture shock that I was to experience in the days ahead.

The Irishman suggested that I spend the night at the hotel where he would be staying, get a night's rest and see if any contacts could be made. If not, I could arrange to return to the states the next day. Weary from the twenty-hour plus flight, a victim of numerous changes of time zones and almost in a state of panic, suddenly it clicked! What about the address of the hostel that the returning missionary had given to me the night before my departure? Could I even locate it, where had I written it? I had been so sure I would not need it. Now I was digging for it like a hungry mongrel desperate for a buried bone. My friend from Ireland asked his driver to attempt to find the location. In my mind, I thought perhaps my new friend was maybe an angel sent from the Lord to aide me in my distress. That impression was short lived as he suggested that we go to a local bar for a few drinks before beginning our search. As I climbed up on the barstool and ordered my coke I wondered what the next step would be.

A RELUCTANT HOST

After a circuitous route and some questions as to directions, we arrived at the hostel. They patiently waited as I knocked on the door of the imposing structure and introduced myself to a gentleman as he opened the door. It was now almost midnight and he was not too sympathetic with my passionate plea for a place to lay my head for the night.

He and his wife were laypersons from Oklahoma, who had volunteered their services to the Foreign Mission Board for a few months while career missionaries were on furlough. He explained that rules and regulations prevented him from allowing me to just appear off the street and request lodging. I showed him brochures I often mailed to pastors in the states, told of my education in Southern Baptist Schools, gave a brief history of past ministry and finally, and with some reluctance, he gave me entrance. Advised that I could only stay for a limited time, I was greatly relieved for the assurance of a night's rest for my weary body.

A WORD FROM GOD FOR A NEEDY SOUL

I could never recall a time in all of my life when I was more discouraged and defeated as I tried to sleep that night. All I could think about was the leadership of God thus far and His providential care. I was embarrassed and ashamed as I considered boarding the plane and returning home without one message preached and facing the friends and churches who had invested financially to make this trip possible. I tossed and turned, wearied almost beyond description, disturbed by the racket of honking horns and loud voices through the night. About 2:00 a.m. I crawled out of my uncomfortable single bed and fell on my knees and tearfully cried out to God. My lament over and over was, "Lord, I am so ashamed." There was no audible voice, but never has God more clearly spoken to my heart with the impression to turn to Psalm 25. I knew Psalm 22, 23, 24 but to save my life I could not tell you what Psalm 25 had to say. As I knelt and wept my eyes fell upon the words of verse nine, *'let me not be ashamed.... the meek will He guide in judgment and the meek will He teach His way.'* The closing words of verse twenty *'let me not be ashamed for I put my trust in thee.'* Instantly peace flooded my heart as God again had shown Himself faithful. With no idea as to how He was going to accomplish it, I knew that He was graciously coming to my rescue and all would be set straight.

The following morning found my host, the volunteer lay missionary, in a more sympathetic mood. As we were discussing the complications of the whole issue before us, there was a knock at the door and a young black man was ushered into our company. He introduced himself as Ado, a true evangelist to his people. Though neatly dressed it was obvious he was extremely poor. I felt ashamed as he explained to me how he would leave his family for weeks and would hitch rides to various parts of his country as he felt impressed of the Holy Spirit. He would venture out with little or no money in his pockets looking for a town in which to preach. He would remain in that city or village until a number of people would be saved and then he would appoint a new convert to serve as pastor of the people. Then it was off to another place of opportunity to repeat the task.

As he shared how he often slept out in the open and prayed for God to daily provide for his food I blushed as I considered how pampered I had been as a so called evangelist. Ado was kind enough to mention that he had preached in the city of Nkawkaw and offered his services in seeking to locate the missing pastor. With some reluctance, the lay missionary agreed to drive us to the city

SEARCHING FOR THE MISSING PASTOR

The following morning we began our venture to find Pastor George Akom-kyie. We boarded the four-wheel drive SUV with me seated next to Karl, my reluctant, temporary host, and Ado sitting just behind me in the rear. Soon after leaving the capitol city of Accra we headed toward the town of Nkawkaw on a road that became progressively more and more narrow and less and less comfortable. Deep potholes were not the exception, but the rule and oncoming traffic reminded me of teenagers playing chicken. No stop signs, no speed limits, no guard rails, it was like a game of guts. As we approached oncoming trucks, buses and autos I could feel Ado's knees pressing against the seat and into my back as he constantly braced for the head on collisions. I don't mind admitting that I was scared out of my wits. My heart and spirit sank as we drove past the little villages of mud brick houses and those built with stick walls and thatched roofs. After about three hours we are at our destination, and searched with little or no success in finding Brother George who had invited me to Africa. I am embarrassed to admit that by this time, I was almost relieved as I wondered if I could remain, sleep and eat in such conditions for nearly two weeks. The poverty was unbelievable, the odors at times were almost unbearable and I could only wonder where I would quarter for those days.

As we began our return trip I was again in a quandary about what I was to do. Driving back on those roads we saw a small boy holding up two large dead gophers, one in each hand and a broad toothy smile on his face. I asked,
"What are those and what is he doing?" Ado answered,
"He is selling them, gophers are fine eating."

As we neared the city I saw huge swarms of bats as they circled trees at sundown. As I voiced my surprise at their numbers and their acrobatic flight I was again informed that before I left I should eat some bat soup. I groaned within and asked why I had placed myself in this position. Lord, where are you?

The following morning I knew nothing to do but to plan to return home with humiliation and shame and then there was a knock at the door. A Ghanaian pastor had come to visit Brother Karl. He introduced himself as Dr. John Aduro and as he learned of my plight he assured me that there was no need to worry. He was pastor of one of the largest churches in the city and he would notify his people of my presence and let me preach in his church. He said, "We will keep you very busy." Karl even agreed to permit me to stay, if I could pay, at the hostel. A joy flooded my heart and I thought to myself, "Lord, surely this was Your plan all along and You have worked your marvelous will and prevented me from having to endure the hardships of those poverty stricken little towns and villages." Little could I have imagined He was again to burst my bubble.

THE LOST IS FOUND

The following morning there was another knock at the door and there stood Brother George with a pastor friend. He shared how he had been at the airport the night I arrived, but could not enter the waiting area for security reasons. As he tried to reach me in the parking area he was also caught in the crush of the men fighting to see who would carry our luggage and he watched as I drove away and had no idea where I had gone. Unbelievably he told us how that in a time of intense prayer the Lord had revealed to him where I was staying and he hired transportation to come and seek me out. To this day I cannot understand all that was involved in this, but I could only believe that the Lord Jesus was again confirming His infinite will for me even if I was not the most comfortable with it at the time.

God continued to unfold His protection for me as I considered the delay in contacting the pastor who had originally extended the invitation to come to Ghana. Had he met me at the airport as planned, I would have immediately been whisked away to the cities of poverty to minister. There would have been no other choice, but to drink the water of the villages, which was at best, less than pure. I was later informed that, without a doubt, I would have experienced serious diarrhea and in all probability very severe and even life threatening ailments. Fortunately, I now left the hostel with four and a half gallons of filtered water to quench the thirst.

As we loaded my supplies into the taxi my host assured me that I would not need the sleeping bag I had brought with me. In the original invitation he had advised me to make sure that one was provided. He now assured me of far better accommodations, the Queen Mother's House in one city and The Japanese Guest House in another. If I had thought that the earlier journey, seeking my host was frightening, I soon was to experience events that would border on terror.

CHAPTER 21

QUARTERING AT THE QUEEN MOTHER'S HOUSE

Relief, that was the word and the emotion that flooded my entire soul, when informed that my week's lodging would be at The Queen Mother's House. The sights of such poverty, the lack of any visible sanitation concerns and the culture shock in general left me with great trepidation.

Ghana for many years had been a British Colony. When Ghana gained her independence, Queen Mothers were chosen to serve as figurehead leaders of particular cities. In my foolish mind, I envisioned the Queen Mother's House would surely be a palace like accommodation and I knew it would be far better than spending my nocturnal bliss in a sleeping bag! I could hardly wait to arrive at our destination.

EVERY HOUR A NEW ADVENTURE

Leaving the safety and security of the Southern Baptist Hostel, my luggage, two and a half gallons of water, and my carcass were wedged into the ancient Datsun taxi, along with the driver and my two host pastors. Packed like sardines, I tried to look comfortable, but mused as to how I could possibly make a three-hour journey without suffocating. Brother George ended the quandary when he explained that we were on our way to a "station" to secure a vehicle to complete our journey to Kukurantumi, our first city of ministry.

A word of explanation is in order to describe, "a station." It can best be envisioned as a place of chaotic disorder. One must remember that Ghana is one of the poorest countries of the world. Bicycles are a luxury and a motorized vehicle is available only to vast minority. If a person desires to travel he does so by foot or by going to a location in a city, a station, where dilapidated cars, vans, open trucks or rattletrap buses gather. I do not exaggerate when I state that most of the vehicles used for such transportation would be found in the junkyards of America. Each time my host pastor would mention going to "the station," to make our way to the next preaching site, fear gripped my entire being.

AT THE STATION

Leaving the hostel, we drive by taxi to the outskirts of Accra and arrive at the station. As we exit the taxi, we are immediately approached by men, women, and boys, scrambling for the opportunity to carry my luggage, which was far too excessive, to the minivan bound for Kukurantumi. A man carries my suitcases and a woman takes one of the water containers in her right hand and places the other on her head, as she walks away, I remember the words of caution from the hostel manager,
"Only use this filtered water for drinking and brushing your teeth." No sooner had the thought entered my cranium than I saw the two-gallon container fall from her head, hit the ground and burst asunder like the bowels of Judas. She was almost in tears, and so was I, when I contemplated almost two weeks left and only two and a half gallons of H2O to quench my thirst.

Finally, we found a Datsun station wagon bound for Kukurantumi and crammed with eight others; we set forth to the first preaching engagement.

A ROYAL RECEPTION

After leaving the hostel in Accra, I was to see only one other white person for more than a week. I mention that only to say that I was an oddity and a celebrity at the same time. As to the celebrity status, I was always given the choice position in every vehicle, the front passenger seat. That might sound like an honor, but it was mainly the suicide location. No seat belts, no guard rails or pavement, a dodge ball mentally as to driving technique, pigs and cows darting from the brushy roadside and pedal to the metal velocity. It is impossible to describe in print the fright that would be my companion for days to come.

After a number of stops, we arrived at the Queen Mother's House. It was a two-story cement structure, much like a small apartment building, left behind by the British Empire. It was quite clean and tidy, compared to all the other facilities of the village. A small entourage met me and led me to a large room for a meeting with the Queen Mother, dressed in her tribal royalty, the tribal chief and other dignitaries. They welcomed me with the reading of a Proclamation and presented a hand woven talisman adorned with the ancestral colors. I was overwhelmed with the reception and with tears brimming my eyes, voiced my deep appreciation, and made the fateful mistake of exclaiming, "You have treated me as if I were President Reagan."

In almost instant chorus, they shook their heads and bellowed, "No, no, not President Reagan." I immediately realized I had stepped in it, recognized they were not Republicans, and became aware of their disdain for Mr. Reagan. Being the quick wit I enjoy, at least I am half right, I responded, "I meant to say, you have treated me like a king", to which there was applause.

A PLACE TO LAY MY WEARY HEAD

I am ushered to my room, my quarters for the next five nights. The room was clean and sparsely furnished, but better than I had expected. There was an indoor commode just down the hall, but no shower. A sponge bath would have to do for a few days. The room came with a servant girl named Sophia, who was blessed with a kind and gentle spirit and one who loved the Lord. Weary from the tiring journey, I longed for a short nap and something to quench my thirst. Sophia hearing my request fetched me a Coke and brought it to my room. She watched as I searched for some way to open the bottle and replied, "Let me open it for you." I stared in amazement as she lifted the bottle to her mouth, placed the cap between her teeth, lowered the bottle and off popped the cap. Grinning from ear to ear, she handed the opened drink and presented it to me. My molars still ache as I picture her feat.

LET THE CRUSADE BEGIN

It was not called a revival, or outdoor meeting; it had been referred to and identified as a crusade. Crude two-by-fours and six-bys and whatever could be gathered and nailed into a makeshift podium and laid on uneven cement blocks; that was the platform. Perhaps a dozen sixty-watt light bulbs were crudely strung around the perimeter of the area, now let the service begin and see the glory fall. The service was to begin at 7:00 p.m. but I was about to be introduced to another cultural reality, time meant nothing to these people. Most did not own nor need a wrist watch; time was relative. Approximately forty-five minutes after seven, Bro. George knocked on my door and informed me it was time to go. As we neared the preaching area, I could hear the music and the people singing, and such singing I had never heard. Such enthusiasm, vibrancy, harmony and the glow of the black faces will forever be sealed in my memory.

DANCING TO A NEW TUNE

Another shock for the set-in-his-ways, ultraconservative, Baptist preacher. Suddenly, the space in front of the platform was cleared and the women formed a circle and began to dance, if you please. Right there, in front of the man of God! I must admit it took me by surprise, but as I watched these poor, joyful saints of God lift their hands and praise Him in song, tears began to flow. For at least twenty minutes they danced, circling the area, clapping, lifting their arms and hands toward heaven, and some shaking tambourines. My mind drifted to many of the churches back in the good ole' USA and I thought of the 'frozen chosen', dead pan expressions, nodding heads that were more concerned with time and tradition than truth and theology, and I shouted, "Glory." Without notice, the women stopped the dance, faded back into the standing crowd and now the men filled the area and in like manner, proceeded to do their spiritual bunny hop. I could not look into their hearts, but my spirit bore witness with theirs, I sensed no grieving of God's Spirit, and I am convinced these were children of the Father, worshipping and praising their Savior in a cultural manner that was all their own. I somehow believe they brought a smile to the face of God who was pleased with their sacrifice.

PREACHNG THE WORD

It is now an hour and half since the service began. I realize that some of these dear people had walked a great distance to be here and they had been standing the entire time. It is my first time to ever stand before such a congregation and I had struggled to determine what to preach. All I knew to do was to proclaim the Cross of Jesus, beginning in Genesis with the sin of Adam and the shedding of the blood and to make our way through the Passover, the Tabernacle and finally to the life and death of our Savior. Preaching for nearly an hour, I observed no person walking away and when the invitation was extended for people to come forward and confess Him as Savior and Lord, many came and my soul was exceedingly blessed.

Making my way to my quarters, I walked with mixed emotions. I was rejoicing because of the eagerness of these dear people to hear the Word of God. My heart ached as I considered their deep poverty with no hope for a better society. I was almost angry when I compared their zeal and love for the Savior and the lukewarm attitude of so many churches in our homeland, and I felt I was at the point of total exhaustion. I had battled insomnia for years as a traveling evangelist, and had not slept well for days, combined with the plague of time change and travel fatigue. I literally cried out to God for the blessing of sleep, but did not find rest until the wee hours of the morning.

As the sun began to rise, I was abruptly awakened by loud, indistinguishable words. It was the amplified prayers of Muslims, crying out from the towers of a local Mosque. I groaned out my complaint to the Father, but to no avail. My time in Kukarantumi was to be set by successive nights of insomnia and days of little rest and yet days of blessings never to be forgotten.

The morning came to say goodbye to the smiling faces of small children and gray headed adults with many bringing gifts. A smiling gentleman placed a full grown goose under my arm, a live chicken under the other and a rotund lady handing me a melon for my lap. These were very best and most sacrificial gifts from the hearts of these followers of the Master. Holding my love offering as tightly as possible, we made our way to our next meeting.

CHAPTER 22

ON TO NKAWKAW

God graciously blessed those days in Kukurantumi and now George tells me it is time to move on to our next 'crusade.' It is with reservation and trepidation we begin this journey. It was the mention of this town that had brought the misgivings of the Southern Baptist missionary who providentially called me the very night before leaving Birmingham for this venture. Also, I have noted how the lay missionary from the hostel and Ado, the Ghanaian evangelist brought me to this city in search of Brother George whom I had missed at the airport. But, I had no choice, so on to Nkawkaw (in-kaw-kaw, no idea what it means).

This time our voyage is via a small, antiquated bus. Same routine, breakneck speed, dusty roads that were too narrow, near head on collisions, and all this and more with me in the seat of honor. Although it was three o'clock in the afternoon, the Harmatan, a phenomenon of fine sand that blew in from the dry Sahara Desert, covered the whole countryside like an early morning fog. You not only see it, but you also taste it and inhale it.

Rattling down the washboard roads, we suddenly stop. Word flows back to our vehicle that there has been an accident just ahead. I step down from the bus and walk a few feet to discover another bus has been forced off the road, passed through some undergrowth, turned over and hurled a man's body to the ground. To my amazement, no one seemed to grieve over the corpse; rather they were upset that the two lanes of traffic were halted. As the people scurried about, uniformed policemen suddenly appeared and with billy clubs swinging, drove them back into the cars and vans. I was nearly knocked to the ground as the people fled. Boarding the bus, I watched with unbelief as six or eight men lifted his body and carried the corpse to the side of a dump truck and tossed his carcass up and over the side like a sack of potatoes. Life appeared to be of little value to the masses that day.

We arrive in the city and as I step off the bus curious children begin to encircle me. Some had never been that close to a white man before. Some venture to rub the hair on my arms. As I stooped down to get on their level, they run their fingers through my curly hair. I become like a Pied Piper and receive a new label,' Obruni,' or, white man. This is a precious photo opt, and opening my camera, I begin to snap some pictures of the smiling, enthralled children. Suddenly, two angry men appear and demand that I cease. One fellow tries to wrestle away my camera. Hey, this is no time to start a scuffle, and in haste I ask George to explain that I was only taking photos of the kids for Jesus. Just as quickly, the anger vanished from their faces, broad smiles appeared and they stood with the children and insisted I include them in the pictures. Whew!

THE JAPANESE GUEST HOUSE

Staying at the Queen Mother's House had been a pleasant experience and knowing of the Japanese as a people of cleanliness, I felt somewhat assured as we made our way to my new residence, The Japanese Guest House. As we descended from the street level, down the steps to the lodging, my heart sank. It was a cement block building, built many years before when some workmen from Japan came to Ghana to install an ancient telephone service. It was seldom used and words of warning were given as we entered the dusty residence, "Brother Bobby, sometimes when buildings are not occupied, one needs to watch for scorpions and cobras!"

Led to my small bedroom, I was introduced to my bed for the week, a small bare mattress on the floor, covered by a dingy blanket. There was an open bathroom with a commode, filthy beyond description, a lavatory and shower, but running water only on certain days of the week and all this with the warning, keep your mouth closed while showering because of contaminated water. But, thank the Lord; I still had my two and a half gallons of filtered H2O.

How I pray that these words are written in seeking to portray this venture, in no way reveal a spirit of ingratitude nor to demean the pastors who invited me. They were providing the very best they had and as pitiful as my accommodations appeared, they were better than any of the faithful men of God enjoyed.

THE PASTORS CONFERENCE

In less than an hour, several pastors and evangelists came to greet me, discuss the open-air services and inform me of the schedule for the week. My heart was so humbled as these men shared with me the testimony of their ministries and the unassuming faith with which they trusted their living God. In the midst of the conversation I made a request for a Coke or some kind of soda. As poverty stricken as the entire culture was, Coca-Cola and Singer sewing machines were advertised in the smallest of and most remote villages. I did not want to appear selfish, but felt I could not share my limited supply of safe water. Handing a young man local currency, he dashed out the door and soon returned with drink, smiling broadly that he had been able to aide this unworthy preacher. And then I did the second most stupid act of the trip. Finding the Coke was unbelievably hot, I asked, "Do you have any ice?" With quizzical looks, they stared at one another and another young man hastened out the door and returned with a small, chipped enamel pan, half filled with ice. Too late, I realized that that small pot represented a real sacrifice to satisfy the whim of a foolish guest. I could not refuse this kindness and proceeded to pour the drink on top of the ice, knowing full well the jeopardy of the contamination of the mixture. Thankfully, I had no ill effects.

"Father, forgive us for showing such ingratitude for the smallest blessings of life."

TREKKING TO THE TASK

A large platform had been erected in an open field on the outskirts of the city. Each night I walked from my room to the services. My course was via the partially asphalted avenue, through the heart of the city. Nightly, I encountered curious stares and experienced near nausea as I passed a certain area of my journey. It was a stifling odor, almost intolerable. I discovered on a daylight jaunt, that there were no public restrooms or outhouses available, so the main street afforded cement troughs on the side of the avenues for the women to stand and straddle to relive themselves, but the males made use of a wall at the end of one corner. It might seem so primitive to our citizenry, but what else could they do? I learned to hold my breath as I traversed that particular area, but again thanked our God for the privileges of the USA.

From a distance, I could already hear the sound of singing, the pounding of drums and the blare of a single trumpet. I have failed to mention that all of this was taking place just days before Christmas and almost the entire country was experiencing a phenomenon called, 'Harmatan.' Harmatan occurred when the north winds blew the sands from the distant Sahara Desert to the countries of the South. It was like the dust storms of the old west. Clouds of small particles hovered over the lighted area of the Crusade field.

PREACHING WITH A BROKEN HEART

Often I have heard the admonition that a preacher should share the Gospel with a broken heart, and likewise the statement, that in every pew there is a broken heart. I did not need a reminder as I preached in Nkawkaw. As I sat on the platform with the pastors, it was all I could do to not weep as I looked out over the several hundred people who stood before me. To stare at such poverty and hopelessness written on the faces of so many and to realize that in a material sense their future was to remain unchanged. To look upon mothers, clutching the infants with little ones at their side, provided scenes I will never forget. Not only was there a broken heart in every pew, though there were no pews, I felt there was a wounded or broken heart in every breast. Never before had I felt such a compassionate urgency to make clear the claims and promises of Jesus.

CHAPTER 23

LONELY IN A CROWD

For five straight nights, our Lord saw fit to bless the preaching of His Word. It was an honor and a challenge to know that you were sharing with some who had never heard the Truth before that week. Only our God knows for sure how many were truly converted, but for me it was a high water event in my life. It was during the long days I became lonely. Most of my hours were spent alone and when I was in the company of my dark skinned brothers, with few exceptions, there seemed to be an invisible barrier that prevented the deepest of fellowship. Language and culture still brought an unexplainable partition. I can promise you it was not prejudice, simply something beyond explanation.

For nearly two weeks now, I had not seen a single white man and in discussion with one of the pastors I was told of a group of white ministers, thought to be Wyclif Bible Translators, were up on the mountain. Expressing my desire to seek these Americans out, Pastor George consented to take me up on the mountain to find them. In our rented taxi, we stopped a dozen times and inquired as to the whereabouts of the white men. Most shook their head and confessed their lack of such knowledge, but one or two encouraged us to go on and upward. I thought about the movie, "Stanley and Livingston," and the long query as to
"Where is the white man?"

Finally, we were directed to a neatly kept house sitting on the hillside. Excitedly, making my way to the front door and knocking, two young men opened the door and graciously bade me enter. To my disappointment, they were not white, but Roman Catholics from Japan leading a ministry called, 'The

Divine Way.' Though extremely gracious and hospitable, they were not hungering for fellowship and after offering a huge glass of cold water, we were on our way back down the mountain.

HOLY TERROR

Several times the fear generated by traveling the roads of Ghana has been noted, but fear was about to be intensified. Without claiming to be the epitome of the macho man, I can honestly say that not a great many things really scare me. But without apology, I admit that my journeys in the vehicles of this country scared the daylights out of me. And now that dread was to be replaced by sheer terror! The taxi that took us up on the mountain was replaced by one of those death trap vans. The driver tossed abandon aside, and like one of Joey Chitwood's Hell Drivers of the 1950's, we descended the mountain like a bat out of Hades. There is no way a description of the expedition could be exaggerated. Countless hairpin curves, huge potholes, deep ravines and not one single guardrail the entire distance. Along the road were several abandoned, burned out vehicles and a glance into the valleys revealed the wreckage of numerous vans and buses, long since forgotten, if ever remembered. I seriously considered the possibility of a like fate and pondered the reality that should I die, no one in the States knew where I was and in all probability Carolyn would never discover what happened to her favorite husband. Every nerve, muscle and fiber of my anatomy was tighter than any guitar string and when we finally reached the station and stepped out of the van, I informed Bro. George that I had made my last trip up the mountain. He kindly rebuked me for my lack of faith and I whispered to myself, "Thou shalt not tempt the Lord Thy God."

NEVER SAY NEVER

It is now Christmas morning, 1986. The meetings in Nkawkaw concluded last night. I arise with a tremendous homesickness. Never have I been away from my family on December 25th. It is with loneliness that I eat my breakfast of a banana, an orange and peanut butter on Ritz Crackers. In preparing for the trip, another word of caution had been given; don't eat the local food, except for fruits that can be peeled. My suitcase had been packed with a jar of crunchy peanut butter, the largest box of Ritz crackers and some packets of pre-cooked meals, vacuum-sealed in foil packages. These, I heated by daily placing them on a hot tin roof. If you are anxious to shed some pounds, I guarantee you this plan will not fail!

The only thing on the menu today is to meet with the pastors for one last conference of encouragement. I needed a word of encouragement far more than I needed to try to boost others, but one never knows what plans our Lord has in mind. As I met with a dozen or so hungry men of God, an older gentleman ambled into the small church. Since it was Christmas, I felt impressed to share with the fellows concerning "The Glory of the Lord" that was manifest to the shepherds on the holy night of our Savior's birth and the desire and design of our Father to reveal that Glory to others through our lives every day. As we closed our lengthy time of fellowship, the elderly gentleman stood by my side, introduced himself and took me aside. Sharing how he had attended the night services, he now wanted to receive Jesus as his own personal Lord and Savior. With our heads bowed, he prayed with repentance and faith and left with rejoicing. I shared in his elation, but only temporarily.

As the pastors milled about the room, one of the older men of God approached me and asked if I had somewhere to preach that night. Already, I had made it a matter of prayer. I really desired to be used at every opportunity and dreaded to go back to my dingy room to spend the day and night by myself. With enthusiasm he shared how much his people would like to hear me, what an honor for a white man to fill his pulpit and on and on. Finally, I interrupted to tell him I would be thrilled to minister to his people. And then I popped the fateful question, "And dear brother, where is your church located?" He replied, "Oh, it is up on the other side of the mountain, we will look for you at seven o'clock tonight." I thought, "Oh, my dear Lord, what have I done?"

FAITH AND FEAR RIDES THE SAME VAN

A couple of fellows accompany me to the 'station' and I feeling like a condemned man walking his last steps to the death chamber. I accept my front seat of honor for the dreaded destination. The van is filled to more than capacity. Regular seats have been removed to replace them with unattached wooded benches to accommodate more passengers. It was now dark, other that the brightness of the moon. Boarding the van, I could not help but notice the trinkets on the cracked dusty dashboard. A collection of small statues of Saints and a crucifix, strands of voodoo beads and teeth hung from the driver's neck, along with a cross. Even before he cranks the engine, he crosses himself for good measure, just in case he has left out any 'unknown god.' For good measure, I, too, bowed my head and silently prayed for the watch care of our Lord.

With appropriate haste, we sped from the dusty station onto the singular paved road. In a few moments we take a sharp right turn onto the winding road leading to the top of the mountain. Could it get any worse? Yes!! I noticed that each time he tapped the dimmer switch on the floor of the van, the headlights would completely go out for a few seconds, with nothing but the light of the moon to guide him, and he never slowed pace. From bright to dim, from dim to bright, out go the headlights. Fright and anger shook hands in my brain. No one seemed concerned, but no fear, for I had enough panic for the entire passenger list.

Finally, after two stops to add water to a steam spitting radiator, George and I reach our destination. Greeted by a number of smiling welcomers, we walk a trail that leads through a poor shantytown with its abysmal paucity and unpleasant aromas. Again, before the small block church building comes into sight, the night seems to vibrate with the voices of the saints, singing their praises to their living, loving, Lord Jesus. I think of that statement, "You will never realize that Jesus is all you need, until Jesus is all you have."

MUSIC TO THE PREACHER'S EARS

The building is packed to capacity, again, a drum is pounded, and a dented trumpet blares out its sweet tune, the people dance with enthralling enthusiasm. For over an hour I watch and listen with amazement and am reminded of the words of Jesus to the church in Smyrna, "I know thy works and tribulation and *poverty* (but thou art rich)." Revelations 2:9.
I realized that I was fellowshipping with spiritual plutocrats and thought of the scarcity of so many churches back home. Oh, if we only knew.

When I speak of music to the preacher's ears, it is not a reference to the joyful singing of the congregation, but to what occurred after the service. I preached for more than an hour. It is now late into the night and when I start to close the service with prayer, an aged man in the back of the building stands and cries aloud, "Can you tell us anything else?" And the people applauded, and I wept. *That music*, was original, and has never resounded again and is still tops on my Hit Parade.

THE THREE-EGG SERMON

It is now past eleven o'clock and I am bone weary, but a man and wife are insistent that we come to their home for a brief visit. With such kindness, they set some food before me, but out of fear of nausea and diarrhea, I try to offer some excuse for not ingesting the kind offer and it appeared my refusal was accepted. I tell Brother George that we must head back to my room and as we rise to leave, the lady of the house weepingly voicing her appreciation for the message that night and explaining she has no money to give, she hands me three raw eggs for a love offering. I smiled as remembered ordering a three-egg omelet at the Waffle House, but this sacrifice was the finest of all. All three cackle-berries placed in my empty hand, how was I to ever get them safely to my room and what could I do with three eggs. George had the perfect solution, give them to him.

THE GRIM DISCOVERY

Making our way back to the station, we stumble through the darkness. It is almost midnight and even the candle lights and lanterns of the small dwellings are snuffed for the night. To my dismay, the station is silent, not one person or vehicle is to be seen. Apologetically, George bows his head and informs me of the obvious, no more transportation for the night. Christmas night and the contemplation of sleeping on the street frustrates and angers me. I think to myself, "How could you be so unaware of the time as we fellowshipped in the pastor's home to place us in a predicament like this," but I kept my mouth shut and trusted God for a solution. He has not failed me yet!

GOODBYE TO THE MOUNTAIN

Assuring me that he will find some mode of transportation, George leaves me and vanishes into the darkness. Such situations makes one a prayer warrior. As I groan out my complaint to the Lord and wonder what God has in store, I hear the racket of an engine, feel the vibrations of a machine without mufflers, and cast my eyes on a pickup truck or what use to be a pickup truck. With a roar that would wake the dead and smoke billowing from beneath the monster, George swings the passenger door open, tells me to get in and he leaps into the bed of the truck filled with yams. No refusals this time of night, I climb onto the bare front seat, with exposed springs puncturing my posterior, and without a moment of hesitation we are on our way down Suicide Mountain. Seeking to show some gratitude and civility, I greet the driver with a smile and an outstretched hand. Without a word of response, he manifested zero desire to communicate. A moment later, I gently quizzed him about how he had enjoyed Christmas Day, and this time there came forth a snarl, indicated he was a Muslim with no interest about my Savior, and certain dislike for Christians from the USA. To further compound the fear, his breath reeked with liquor and later I discovered that George had bargained with him in a local bar.

(I realize the repetition of these like experiences grows tedious in reading, but fourteen years later they still remain so vivid in my memory and are an important part of God working in my life to build faith for future times of struggle.)

Prayer, voodoo dolls or Christian crosses did not initiate *this* journey. With unexplained anger he jerked the rattletrap truck into gear and sped away with fierceness. Not only were there no floor mats, the metal floorboard revealed gaping holes, and I could not only see the flames coming from the exhaust manifold, I could feel the generated heat. I actually turned on my cassette recorder to document the deafening roar of the engine. Of all the excursions up and down the mountain, this was the most terrifying. Upon arriving at my quarters, I again vowed to George, God, and myself that I would not travel from another station. I could not have been more sincere had I written it in my own blood.

AN OASIS IN THE WILDERNESS

Although looked upon as one of little faith, Brother George finally succumbed to my demand of better transportation and the staunch refusal to put my life at risk by agreeing to take part in another demo derby. We make out exit from Nkawkaw on a real National Bus with actual space for luggage, extra seats and not one single chicken, goat, goose or any like varmint.

Three hours later we arrive in the small town of Kumasi. I was introduced to a young pastor, Brother Robert, and informed I was to go to his home to await a taxi that would carry me to a small university where I would have lodging for the night. While waiting at Brother Robert's home, curious children began to gather on the steps, smiling and pointing at the peculiar 'Obruni', the white man. Returning their smiles, they moved closer and soon engulfed me, again rubbing the hair on my arm and touching the waves of hair on my head. They sang and quoted Scripture and reveled in the opportunity to be so close to an 'Obruni.'

This was the very first time I saw toys that were not just handmade, but little dolls from the States, clutched as tightly as a newborn babe. Even though I had encountered and daily witnessed the severe abject poverty of the populace, it never became routine or ordinary to me. My heart grieved for all the people, but especially for the children. It all seemed so hopeless and futile.

Robert had never sought to explain his absence, but in due time he returned to his home by taxi and apprised me of the plans for the day. He was to take me to the small university, help me unpack and come back that night for an evening service in a local church. As we approached the campus, it was far from what had been described as a suitable place to lodge, even for two nights. Suddenly, the Lord brought to my weary recollection, the mention of a Southern Baptist Seminary, during that providential phone call from Gene Covington the night before I left the states. I remembered that he had told me of its existence in the little town of Kumasi. As kindly and as humbly as possible, I asked Robert if he would help me locate that institution. With the benevolence and grace that characterized almost every pastor I had encountered, he pledged his aide to fulfill my request. After a couple of stops and inquiries, he smilingly informed me that it was no problem to meet the desires of my heart.

Two phrases I often heard in Ghana that meant absolutely nothing were "no problem" and "not far." Usually those words indicated a long journey and many complications. We must have driven at least twenty-five miles to arrive at the 'not far' seminary, but what a relief to drive into the yard of a small white blockhouse, a dwelling with a well-kept lawn and flowers surrounding the abode. Not knowing what the reception would be, I walked to the door and gently knocked. Momentarily the door flung open revealing a distinguished lady, Margie Verner, and without hesitation she invited me into her home. Summarily, describing my circumstances, she greeted me with a hug and assured me of my welcome into their lovely residence. In another moment, her husband, Dr. Gene Verner, president of The Ghana Baptist Seminary, entered the home and extended a warm greeting and strong handshake.

My simple vocabulary is too limited to describe the sheer elation of my soul that afternoon. Without one iota of prejudice, my heart rejoiced in being able to sit down with those with whom I could communicate and meet individuals who had ministered to these people for many years and understood the culture shock I had experienced for two solid weeks. Recognizing my weariness and fatigue, the result of days and days without a good night's sleep, they encouraged me to shower and catch a nap before an early supper. It was an absolute luxury to step into a squeaky clean shower and enjoy hot and cold running water, and I didn't even have to keep my mouth closed for fear of ingesting the contaminated flow. Never have I ever showered and shampooed and soaked for that length of time. And then to crawl between crisp, white, lightly starched sheets with no fear of bugs, spiders, scorpions or snakes, it was joy beyond description. In moments I was in dreamland and then the knock on the door, "Brother Bobby, supper is ready." Not peanut butter and crackers, no warm pouch of vacuum sealed beef and noodles, but fresh meat, vegetables, rice and bread, a huge glass of real iced tea. It was an oasis in the desert, a little bit of heaven, and a place of physical, emotional and spiritual rejuvenation. Moments that will never be forgotten.

Brother Robert arrived at the door to ferry me to a small fellowship of believers and believe it or not, the service actually began on time. I was delivered back to the seminary by

9:00 p.m. and sat down with the Verners and fellowshipped past midnight. I was almost embarrassed at my verbosity, but felt I must share my joys and disappointments with my journey. It was such an encouragement to hear of their like experiences in the early days of their arrival in Ghana and they marveled at my ability to handle the situations I had faced, especially being thrust into such a culture alteration with no preparation. Over and over I expressed my deep appreciation for the hospitality afforded a stranger out of nowhere and made my way to that wonderful inner spring mattress, clean sheets and a spotless room.

Amazing what a good night's sleep can do for a weary soul. I actually slept until 7:00 am. No honking horns, no loud cries at daylight to Allah, just awaking to chirping birds and the sounds of nature. Margie called us to a breakfast fit for a king. There was fresh fruit, sausage, buttered toast and hot coffee. Common, yes, but never more appreciated and another keen reminder of how much we take for granted and how routine our blessings before a meal can become.

CHAPTER 24

ALL GOOD THINGS MUST COME TO AN END

Never have I left a residence with such regret. My desire was to build a tabernacle and remain at my haven, but God knew it was time to go back into the valley. Brother Robert arrived at ten o'clock to make our way to another church in the city. The service began at eleven and as usual the saints sang, danced and testified until twelve-thirty. By now I was accustomed to the tradition and patiently waited until the preaching time and shared the Word for an hour. Again, no one left the service; in fact, the people were still enjoying fellowship when we left a half-hour later.

Leaving Kumasi, we were to make our way back to Nkawkaw, gather all my belongings and go to our last preaching opportunity in the town of Kofuduria. Arriving in Nkawkaw, we were appalled to find that Brother George was nowhere to be found. The Japanese Guest House was locked and only George had the key. Robert was broken hearted and I was angry. When he did finally arrive it was too late for us to get to the church in Kofuduria to preach that night. Robert was saddened that his people would be gathering to hear the "white man", and I was angry that his tardiness made it necessary to spend another night in the Guest House, but I tried to rest in the assurance of His Providence and Sovereignty.

ONE LAST SHOCK

As usual, I am awake at daylight, get up and pack for the last time and await George's six-thirty arrival. I ought to know better by now, but I have always been a slow learner. He arrives without apology at seven-thirty and we make our way to the station. Per my demand, we board a small, gaily painted old bus. The vehicle is packed and there are the usual geese, goats, etc. We rumble our way though the villages along washboard roads, but thankfully, no mountains and the bus is too dilapidated for swiftness.

As on several occasions, we come to soldiered checkpoints. Because of political instability, fear of civil uprisings, etc., when one travels from one district to another, these checkpoints are fairly routine, but not today. Swinging iron gates block the roadway, vehicles come to a stop and an armed lawman boards the bus and walks down the aisle, usually with glares of authority. Today is to be different. When he comes to me, the white man, he tells me to get my luggage and 'step down', meaning get off the bus. He demands that I open my suitcases on the ground and with the muzzle of an AK 47, he begins tossing my personal effects aside. When he sees my gallon zip lock pouch filled with all kinds of prescription medications, he asks for an explanation. With fear and trembling I try to explain all my ailments and the need for heart, blood pressure, gout, and all the others to the grim armed guard, but I find little sympathy. Gruesome thoughts of imprisonment for the transportation of illicit drugs race through my mind. He calls another soldier to his side and they heatedly exchange words. Finally, George makes a lengthy impassioned plea on my behalf and I am told to repack my bags and get back on the bus. Again, I consider what would have happened if I had been tossed in jail? In reality, no one back home knew where I was and I pondered if Carolyn would have ever known what had happened to her first husband?

SWEET FELLOWSHIP AND GREAT SADNESS

My last preaching engagement was one of great joy and sadness of heart. The service was on a Sunday morning and for whatever reason, the people appeared to be more prosperous than in any other church where I ministered. Arriving early, I was met by a small group of precious little girls, attired in neat dresses and little bonnets. I knelt in front of them and asked them to quote verses of Scripture and they were jubilant in response. "Will you sing some songs for me?" I asked, and smiling at one another, they burst into chorus with melody fit for the ears of angels. I could not restrain the tears as I realized that the theme of most of their refrains were about the longing for the return of Jesus. I realized afresh that hardship, persecution and poverty cause one to look for the Blessed Hope! I wondered, what will it take for America to stand on tiptoe and look toward the heavens?

Wherever I went, the customs rarely altered, energetic praise to God in song, testimonies for the blessings from God and dancing that surely won the smile of the Savior. It is with mixed emotions I stand to preach for the last time in Ghana. So many difficulties and yet so many rich experiences that will forever endure and remained etched in my memory. Again, I am privileged to exhort and comfort for over an hour and at the conclusion, the saints offer such words of appreciation. And then, the heartache...

Everyone finally leaves the building and a little boy of ten hangs around until he and I are alone. Dressed in his Sunday best, he asks me if I will go aside and pray in private with him. We find a small empty classroom and he introduces himself as David. I can tell that his heart is deeply burdened and he seems to be reluctant to share his request with me. Finally, he begins to softly weep and open his heart. His request, "Brother Bobby,

I wet the bed every night and my father punishes me. He heard that the 'white man' is coming to preach and he said, "I want you to go and ask him to heal you."

(After almost twenty-five years, I weep as I write these words.) I thought, if David lived in the USA his family could take him to an urologist, be given a prescription and cease to be scolded, beaten and humiliated. We knelt together and I laid hands of him and prayed with a fervency I had seldom known. I pled and begged the Father for his healing. He went his way and I mine, never knowing the result, but to this day little David's face and his expectations of the 'white man' still haunts me. I long to see him in Heaven, finally healed, and living in great wealth!

PREPARATIONS FOR HOME SWEET HOME

Still chafing, somewhat, for my lack of faith, George arranges for the final leg of my journey. Accepting, but not appreciative of my distinct disdain for suicide vehicles available at the 'station', we, (I), pay for a private auto, a 1983 Peugeot, to transport me from Kofoduria to Accra. The auto might have been more reliable, but the driver was in no way more reasonable when it came to cautiousness or prudence in driving habits. Same pedal to the metal mentality and absolutely no evidence of fear. I am convinced that the fatalism of Islam has been transferred to every area of life for many of these dear people, and it has even affected the philosophy of some Christians who consider such as faith.

It is with the full gratitude and relief of my soul when we arrive at the Baptist Hostel and are greeted by the volunteer missionaries from Oklahoma, Brother Carl and his wife. I am sorry to confess that no tears are shed as I watch Brother George and the Peugeot drive off into the sunset.

The dormitory type rooms at the hostel had seemed to be quite rustic and inadequate when I had first arrived in Ghana, but now they appeared to be something of a luxury. Clean sheets, a clean room, hot and cold running water, all reminded me of how I had carelessly looked on such amenities with an unappreciative attitude of gratefulness, but hopefully never again.

As we sit down for our evening meal, I again find myself gushing forth the details of recent days like an artesian well. I am not looking for sympathy or compliment, but I suppose it was of some therapeutic relief. The missionary couple kindheartedly listened to the whole discourse, but their faces seemed to reflect, "You should have known better than to accept the invitation of one Ghanaian pastor, one whom you did not know and had absolutely zero knowledge concerning his circumstances."
And humanly, they were exactly right, but I could see the Hand of God in every occasion.

THE FINAL LEG

It is December 29, 1986. Karl and I are headed for the International Airport in Ghana. He warns me afresh of the mob scene we are about to encounter as we pull into the parking area. Men and boys run a foot race behind the SUV, pushing and shoving to determine who will carry the luggage to the terminal. As head of the hostel, he has been through this routine many times, but admits one never becomes accustomed to the bedlam. He vividly describes the fistfights he has seen erupt and advises me to let him handle the whole situation.

Finally, two of the huskier fellows win out and receive their tips with smiling gratitude. There still remains muddled confusion as to my Visa and Passport and now I am directed to the final corridor toward the KLM 747. But alas, one more bit of nail biting as I am led into a small curtained room for a body check, a strip search. It was a humbling experience and somewhat unsettling because part of the investigation was to determine if I had spent any US currency, which would have been illegal. Ah, the welcome words, "Move on," were music to my ears.

With relief I board the flight and nestle in the comfort of the extra wide, plush, business class seats, and silently shout Halleluiah as I hear the roar of the engines and rumble down the runway. Moments later I hear the thump of the landing gear fold into the wings of the giant jumbo jet, and finally inhale the cool air with no dust of the Harmatan. Home might still be many thousands of miles away, but I was headed in the right direction.

WHY?

Why this excursion? Why did I go? What was the purpose of it all or was there really a reason for this two-week jaunt? I had not been in the air very long before God's Spirit began to speak to my heart with great clarity. "My son, the intention of the voyage was not for them, it was for you." And though hundreds had responded to the simple presentation of the Gospel and scores of individuals had voiced appreciation for the messages of encouragement, I knew that our Heavenly Father had nailed me with that truth. He permitted my ignorance to show Himself Sovereign and strong for my personal, spiritual benefit.

As I noted at the very beginning of this lengthy interlude, my personal conviction is that the most important, the most valuable and vital spiritual asset of the believer is faith. Faith is no more and no less than that God given ability to trust Him to do all that He says He will do. That Divine asset is never to become stagnant, but is to be constantly purified and stretched to new dimensions, and this is only accomplished through heart knowledge of the Word and being allowed to walk through deep valleys of testing and trial. As this ability to trust God grows incrementally, we are enabled by the Lord to totally and confidently face the ever-increasing difficulties with the knowledge that He did it before, and He will do it again. It is with no attitude that considers myself as one who has arrived, but this experience was pivotal in bringing a new level of assurance in my heart that you can depend on God. As I rehearse how He so providentially and with Sovereignty ruled in the smallest of details, even as I viewed some of them as calamities, I was more prepared to face crushing events in future days.

I pray that these words do not reveal a spirit of haughtiness, but to see all of God's disciplines as stepping stones, preparing us to face the next valley. "When darkness seems to hide His face, we rest on His unchanging Grace. We dare trust the sweetest frame, but wholly lean on Jesus Name. On Christ the Solid Rock we stand, all other ground is sinking sand." Amen and Amen.

CHAPTER 25

THE INNER CITY MINISTRY

With vision restored by means of a lens implant, I now found myself waiting on the Lord for His direction for my life. A few revival invitations came, but not enough to supply our financial needs. As I supplied in a number of pulpits, I was invited to speak at the Fourth Avenue Baptist Church located in the inner city of Birmingham. The former pastor had resigned after nearly forty years of service and the church that had averaged over 200 people was now having less than seventy-five in attendance. So-called 'white flight' had taken a real toll on the neighborhood and any promise of real growth was hardly an expectancy. In a matter of weeks, the people extended a call for me to come as their pastor. I must admit it was an agonizing decision. The people were super folks, but the thought of becoming the pastor of a fellowship in a dying community was not appealing. There was a struggle with my own sinful ego that said, 'surely a person of my experience deserved a better place of service.' I am so ashamed to write those words and admit the rottenness of my old sin nature, but God knows and you might as well know it too.

Another shameful admission is that I felt the former pastor had, perhaps, given up to the situation and had not done enough to reach out to all the people of the community, white and black alike. The night the church voted on my call to come as pastor, I told them I would come on the condition that they would permit me to knock on every door of the surrounding homes and that they would welcome every born again person into the fellowship regardless of color. They voted unanimously for me to come as their pastor.

I came to that fellowship with the same philosophy of ministry. I gave myself to hours of study and preparation, believing that sixty people deserved the same diligence in preaching as six hundred. Day by day, I ventured into the neighborhood, knocking on doors at random, sharing God's simple plan of salvation. Not once was I received with rudeness, but seldom with great enthusiasm. We saw a number of children come to Christ, but few adults. The adults that did come to our services did not remain. It was with difficulty I came to understand that there was a definite difference in culture and worship style, and any outreach to the African-American community seemed all but futile. Some of the more charismatic churches were having success in integrating their fellowships, but not us.

An illustration that reveals something of the culture of the neighborhood occurred as I visited from door to door. One day as I rang the doorbell of a particular home, the door opened slightly and a gentleman asked the reason for my visit. On informing him that I was the pastor of the church around the corner, he replied, "I have seen you going about knocking on doors and I told my wife you must be a man of God, for I surely would not do what you are doing for fear of my life." His statement was somewhat exaggerated, but it was a high crime area and I feel sure I had underestimated the danger of doing what I was doing. I do know that more than one parent told me that they would not let their children play outdoors because of their fear of harm to those kids. It was not just a place of 'white flight', but also a community where African-American families were leaving whenever possible.

No pastor could ask for a more kind, congenial congregation of believers, but there was a constant struggle with my ministry there. I am sure there was some ego involved, but having served as an evangelist and pastoring a church in a growing community, baptizing more than eighty people a year, it was now difficult to adjust to a situation where the church had long since peaked and the community was now in a state of slow decline. But I knew that the Lord had led me there and I was committed to stay until He opened another door. When people asked me how the work was going at Fourth Avenue, I would smile and say the church was dying slower than any church I had ever served.

A STEP OF FAITH

After five years of ministry at Fourth Avenue, I felt that God was now bringing that same sense of restlessness to my heart and that a change was to soon take place in my life. As stated before, I have never had difficulty in sensing the Lord's leading to a particular ministry, but there has always been a real struggle in resigning from a place of service. After months of seeking His face about the decision, I resigned as pastor in December of 1997 to again enter the ministry of revival, evangelism and Bible conference engagement. It was not an easy decision. I was now sixty years old, no meetings were scheduled and resigning the church meant no income at all. Amazingly, the Lord began to open the doors of opportunity and I had contacted our Foreign Mission Board about spending time in Third World Countries. I was thrilled with the new challenge and anxious to again be involved with the initial calling God had placed on my heart.

CHAPTER 26

THE DARK VALLEY MINISTRY

One of my first invitations was to teach the Book of Ephesians in a church in Shelby County. Although I had preached through this rich book more than once and had read it dozens of times, I felt compelled to dig deep into its treasures again. The first chapter of the epistle came alive with new insights. As I read and pondered how He picked us, predestinated us, purchased us, provided us with enlightenment and protects us by the sealing of the Holy Spirit, it suddenly leaped off the page that all of this was and is to reveal *HIS* GLORY. (His glory is all that He is and all that He does.) Truly it is all about Him and not about us. As I studied, it became so consuming that He is working all things toward His praise. I had known this, but in reality I had not known it. Little did I realize that this fresh revelation was to prepare me for the most difficult and devastating experience of my life and ministry.

During those days of preparation I had not felt well and each day brought progressive weakness. Ron Dunn, a sweet and blessed friend, was in Birmingham one week and we had the opportunity of great fellowship. Ron was dealing with a serious sinus infection and my symptoms were similar, so I diagnosed myself with the same ailment. But then, I began to experience massive nosebleeds that required cauterizing of the nostrils.

The following Sunday, I began the Bible study. The next night I apologized for my weakness and sat down for the two-hour study. Tuesday night was even more difficult and on Wednesday I called my doctor for an appointment. When I walked into his office, I said, "Doc, (pardon the expression) I don't feel worth a snot."

After a thorough exam, including blood samples, he did not have an explanation. He said to wait on the test results. Carolyn and I returned home and made preparations for our final night of the study of Ephesians. Shortly, the phone rang and upon answering, a lady introduced herself and informed me that a problem had been found and that I was to immediately come to the emergency room at Montclair Hospital and be admitted. Shocked, I asked her the reason for the request and she hesitated to give an answer. I informed her that I did not mean to be rude, but that I was not coming to the hospital without an explanation. Her answer made my blood run cold, "Mr. Britt, it appears that you are experiencing kidney failure and it is of utmost importance that you come to the hospital as soon as possible."

I groaned as I sat back in my chair, fear immediately gripped my entire being and tears began to brim my eyes. It was if a movie was passing through my mind and I was watching vivid scenes of one of my closet friends fight the losing battle with kidney failure and dialysis. Daryl Jones had become my best friend at Howard College. We spent countless hours fishing together, going to Southern Baptist Conventions and Conferences. He later became my pastor. He developed kidney disease and I watched him slowly deteriorate as complications developed over the next few years and I watched my very best friend die by degrees. In a moment I remembered how his life and ministry became more and more limited and then his death and the sorrow and grief that filled my heart when I preached his funeral. I could hardly relay the message to Carolyn as she questioned the substance of the phone call from the hospital.

It was late that afternoon, when we were admitted to the hospital. A plethora of tests were made and in a few hours it was determined that my kidneys had indeed failed. We learned some days later that a rare disease, called Wegner's Disease, had killed the kidneys. A kind and gracious urologist came into my room with the diagnosis and offered words of advice and encouragement, assuring me that a kidney transplant would be possible and then asked if he could have prayer with Carolyn and me. His assurance of a future transplant was a great encouragement, but little did I comprehend the fearsome road that lay ahead until that reassurance would become a reality.

In a couple of days, tubes were placed into my body just above the left collarbone. The next day I was ushered into a small ward for my first dialysis treatment. My family stood at the door and watched as I was hooked up to a coke machine sized apparatus and the four-hour process began. Dialysis is a method whereby one of the implanted tubes lets blood flow out of the body into the machine and goes through a filtering system to remove the toxins and the excess fluid that failed kidneys can no longer do on their own. On the bed next to me was a fellow whose stomach was distended three times its normal size and I wondered if that was to become my fate in the months to come.

Those two weeks in the hospital were a contradiction in experience. I have never known a greater sense of the presence of our Lord; the Word became alive as I opened its pages. And yet there were moments of depression, anxiety and fear. I was dismissed from the hospital and returned home so weak I could hardly stand. The following day we made our way to a dialysis center for my first treatment since the hospital. It was a cold, rainy afternoon and as I was being introduced to this new lifestyle, a nurse informed me that my favorite book of the Bible was to become the Book of Job. I am sure she meant to encourage me, but if so, her statement certainly missed the mark. At the conclusion of the treatment I could not stand because my blood pressure bottomed out. I was given some salty broth and shortly placed in a wheel chair to return home. My heart hurt for Carolyn as she had to sit in a waiting area for over four hours and I realized this was to be our lifestyle for three days each and every week for the rest of our lives unless God came to our rescue with a miracle. It was about eight o'clock that night as we made our way home. I broke down and sobbed as we plowed through the cold February rain. I turned to Carolyn and asked, "What in this world have I gotten us into?" That night was one of the lowest moments of my entire life.

WALKING THE VALLEY

There had been those times of testing and discipline in my life, but all of them had been temporary, fairly short in duration and certainly not debilitating. But now comes this trial that will prove to be long-term and perhaps terminal. Some individuals handle dialysis quite well and I observed a small number of people who were able to receive the three times a week procedure and go to the place of their business, but I soon discovered that I was not going to be able to tolerate that lifestyle very well. Most of the time I would leave the center almost too weak to walk. I would call Carolyn and ask her to meet me in the driveway and assist me into the house. She would have to undress me and I would go to bed for a couple of hours. More than once I would drop to my knees in the shower and call for her to help me to my feet. I would feel better the following day, but then it was back to the center and begin the cycle over again.

There were times when life was fairly normal and I could ride and play a round of golf or go bass fishing, but I always finished totally depleted of energy. A person on dialysis was very limited as to diet and had to be constantly on guard not to drink too much liquid fluid because of the inability to eliminate enough urine from your body. I have lost as much as six pounds during a four-hour treatment.

A NEEDED LESSON ABOUT EMPATHY

One of the most difficult problems I had to deal with was those moments and hours of depression. Before my own personal experience with this agonizing malady, I was too prone to say to those who battled that dark enemy,
"Hey man, get over it. Quit feeling sorry for yourself!"
I came to understand it is like telling a person to just get over cancer or paralysis. I can now identify with those poor souls who live in the grips of this monster and have sympathy for their condition.

Another experience that compounded this melancholy was that of seeing others go through their misery. A dialysis center becomes a little community and in that group of people you get to know individuals by name and enjoy their friendship. A large percentage of the patients are diabetic and this results in major complications. A fellow comrade would not show up for treatments for a couple of days and in asking about their absence I would be informed that they were in the hospital having a toe removed. In months to come, as the disease progressed, it was a foot or a leg that had to be amputated. Some patients were transported to the center by ambulance and others were in such condition that they groaned out their agony for long periods of time. On at least two occasions individuals died during their treatments. Now, though these were the exceptions rather than the rule, they did make depression a frequent visitor to my house. I thank God, though this dark enemy repeatedly made his dreaded appearance, my bouts were fairly short lived occasions.

I pray that these recollections do not leave the impression that life was unbearable and that all was misery; far from it. Our Lord was teaching me things about His Grace and sufficiency that made the five years of dialysis worth the trip. I continued to preach a few revival meetings, fill the pulpit of a number of churches and served as interim pastor in two wonderful fellowships. In time, I was able to leave the three times a week to the center for dialysis and began treatments at home engaging a new procedure called peritoneal dialysis. Without going into great detail as to a description of this home treatment, it freed me up to travel, go to our lake house without returning to a center and made life much more enjoyable. Although peritoneal dialysis did involve carrying a large quantity of supplies, two large boxes of fluid, a heavy tabletop machine, it was like a release from prison.

CHAPTER 27

SUFFICIENT GRACE

I can appreciate the words of Paul in the Book of Romans when he says there are those times when "we do not know how to pray as we ought."

Without a doubt, I continued to cry out to Him for healing, but in those five years of dialysis, I never received a word from Him that that was His will for my life. I am sure that there are those who would rebuke me and say that is exactly why I was not healed. I simply did not claim it by faith. There had been too many times in my life when our Lord made clear to me His will in certain matters and then I could boldly claim His revealed will for my life. I knew that healing was to come, either by the coming of the Lord Jesus when we shall be made like Him or through death or His instantaneous touch to my body or through a kidney transplant. But, that which was and is most important, I cried out to Him for His divine enablement, grace, that Christ would be revealed through this entire experience. I realized that when I was weak, it gave Him an opportunity to reveal His strength. I pray that this does not sound or appear as prideful boasting or spiritual superiority, but many people marveled and laid undeserved compliments at my feet, voicing appreciation as to how I was handling the situation. It was an opportunity to not only preach and theoretically speak of His sufficiency, but to actually experience and live each day with and by that grace.

DAYS OF BLESSED OPPORTUNITY

Churches that are without a pastor and are seeking a new minister usually call someone to serve as Interim Pastor. Agape Baptist Church called me to serve in that capacity for almost a year. Knowing of my physical condition, they only asked me to preach twice on Sunday and Wednesday night with no responsibility for counseling and other pastoral expectations. It was a great fellowship and the necessity of study and preparation offered a welcomed challenge. Unless a person is driven by God's call to preach, he cannot appreciate the fulfillment and joy that comes in delivering His Word. One of the subtle temptations I have always faced is that of loving to preach more than loving the Lord whom I preach. Blessed days, indeed, were those spent at Agape Baptist.

Some months later, I received a phone call from the chairman of deacons of Palmerdale Baptist Church, a small community just outside of Birmingham. He called to ask me if I would preach the following Sunday, explaining that they were without a pastor and were seeking an Interim. It was kind of like a trial sermon, in that they would hear me, and if they were impressed and felt it was God's will, they would call me. The Lord be praised, the church did call us to come and serve in that capacity. Again, with great sympathy, the only expectation was that of preaching twice on Sunday. It was a tremendous blessing, attendance increased and a number of people were saved and others joined the church. I felt like that fellow who walked into the post office and saw his picture on display, and made the comment, "It is wonderful to feel wanted."

While serving at Palmerdale, my physical condition worsened. I was increasingly becoming weaker and having some difficulty with congestive heart failure. Fairly often, it was necessary for me to sit, rather than stand, while preaching.

A very special deacon, and friend, purchased a high backed bar stool to meet that need. That bar stool is now in our little garden home almost ten years later and I will explain its significance later. The days at Palmerdale were glorious days, indeed. The people were so opened to the Word, so gracious in their compliments and generous in their honorarium. Though it was far too long for an Interim Pastor, we served there for three years.

CHAPTER 28

THE UNSEEN HAND OF GOD

It was during those wonderful days at Palmerdale that our Sovereign Lord began to reveal Himself in ways totally unexpected and unexplainable. And we should not be surprised, for that is how He usually does His glorious work. I often say He seldom comes through the front door, but usually through a side entranced.

Carolyn and I were and are members of the First Baptist Church in Trussville, but seldom were in attendance because of service in other churches. While still at Palmerdale, my pastor, Gary Hollingsworth, asked if I would preach in his absence, while he attended a Pastors Conference in Jacksonville, Florida. After asking permission to be absent from Palmerdale, I leaped at the opportunity. I wanted to express our appreciation to the people at First Baptist for lifting us in prayer and secondly, my vanity looked forward to preaching to 1,200 people rather than 100 people at Palmerdale.

ANOTHER HURDLE

Two weeks before the scheduled service at First Baptist Trussville, I became quite ill. The problem was diagnosed as gall bladder infection that demanded immediate surgery. During the surgery, it was discovered that the bladder had become gangrenous and ruptured. Of course this would make recovery a bit more difficult and threatened my opportunity to preach in our home church. On the Saturday night before the Sunday morning I was to speak, I experienced terrible nausea and vomiting. Little sleep was enjoyed that night and Carolyn urged me not to attempt to preach, but I was determined to share God's Word. Perhaps the person who defined a sermon as 'that with which a fellow will get out of the bed with a 104 degree temperature and preach what he wouldn't walk across the street to hear was right.

The kind deacon from Palmerdale, Joe Denton, had brought the bar stool to First Baptist, just in case I needed it. By the grace of God, I dressed that morning and made my way to the church to preach. By this time, my complexion was ashen and my voice was weak and about three octaves above normal. As I stood to preach, I apologized to the people, mentioning my recent surgery, but never alluding to my kidney problem, dialysis or any other ailment. I sensed great liberty that morning and the people offered their kind words of compliment, but unbeknown to me, something was taking place that only our Living Lord could accomplish. Seated toward the back of the auditorium was a young lady whom I had never met. She was not overly impressed by the guest preacher that morning, and had decided to not return to the evening service that night. Fortunately her plans were interrupted when a friend called and asked her to take a special prayer request to the singles fellowship that met each Sunday following the night service. Not wanting to disappoint her friend, she agreed to fulfill her request.

After I had preached that night, this twenty-five year old young lady attended the singles fellowship. After activities and refreshments were concluded, they gathered for a time of prayer. Someone asked about the health of the sickly looking preacher that had filled the pulpit that day. As only God could arrange it, a lady who lived in our garden home community was there. She explained the problem of my kidney failure and added that she felt I would not live much longer without a transplant. As they prayed about the needs of others and my need, it came her time to pray. As she prayed for the puny looking preacher, she felt that the Lord spoke to her and said, "Why don't you give him one of your kidneys?"

The next morning, Ashley called Carolyn to tell her of her experience and inquired as to what she needed to do in order to become a donor. Obtaining the phone numbers at The University of Alabama, Birmingham the wheels began to turn. The minutia of events that followed gave clear evidence that God was in control.

After making an appointment with the donor center, she began to make plans for the testing process to see if she was a match. At that time, Ashley was serving as an athletic trainer for Pinson Valley High School. She had a Masters Degree in Sports Medicine. First on her list was to engage a substitute teacher and give instructions as to the subject that was to be taught. As she randomly opened her manual, she was shocked to see it was a chapter on organ donors. She relates that as she was driving to UAB, a bumper sticker caught her eye that read, "Don't take your organs to heaven, heaven knows we need them here", and then a billboard with the same instruction. On arriving at the hospital and finding the office of the physician who was to make the needed tests, she was amazed to see all of the diplomas and awards honoring the doctor, identifying him as Dr. Fisher. That 'just happened' to be her last name, Fisher, Ashley Fisher. Just happened? Don't you believe it! God was affirming His will for her life and mine.

THE BLESSED INTRODUCTION

It is now Tuesday night, and the telephone is ringing. On answering, I hear the sweet voice and she is telling me how God is leading her to make the tremendous sacrificial gift to a sixty-five year old codger like me. I wept as she described the events of the last Sunday and how she had been tested and found to be a perfect match as a donor. Her words were a total surprise to me because Carolyn had not told me of her phone call the day before, fearful that I would get my hopes up, only to see them crash to the ground. She felt that in all human likelihood, Ashley would not be a suitable donor. The tears flowed as she shared her testimony with me and how excited she was about her desire to give me one of her kidneys. After a lengthy conversation, I interrupted to tell her that I could not, in good conscience accept her offer. Voicing my profound appreciation, I shared how that I was sixty-five years old and had seen and experienced what most people would not in two lifetimes. I related to her that as a twenty-five year old young lady, it would not be fair for her to make such a sacrifice. I spoke of her marriage one day, and how she did not need the scaring of her body at this stage of her life. Not to be put off so easily, she asked if she come to our home the following night. Again, it just *'happened'* to be Valentine's Day when she rang the doorbell that Wednesday evening. She entered with a platter of cookies and a charming smile. Sitting down, she began again to express her desire to offer me the kidney that would save my life. Interrupting her, I wept as I voiced my profound appreciation for her courage and unbelievable generosity, but continued to decline the offer. Kindly, but abruptly, she interrupted, "Brother Bobby, this is not about you and me, this is a God thing, and I know this is what God wants me to do."

With that, my argument ceased and all we three could do was to sob with joy unspeakable and anticipate what our Heavenly Father would do in the coming days. By the way, we later learned that not only was this Valentine's Day, it was also Organ Donor Appreciation Day. Friend, you will never convince me that our God and Savior is not in complete control of our lives and the entire universe included. Our God reigns! What a mighty God we serve.

CHAPTER 29

PREPARING FOR THE TRANSPLANT

Preparation for the surgery was not a simple one, two, three procedure. One issue is that of choosing a date that is compatible with Ashley's work schedule. The last of May is decided upon in order for her to have adequate healing time during the summer months. A battery of tests must be performed to insure that she is a proper candidate. She must be evaluated psychologically and physically. This will include a three day stay in the UAB hospital for arteriograms, cat scans, etc. to make sure her kidneys are in good shape and that her heart is healthy. To say the least, these are anything but comfortable procedures. Psychological examinations are in order to make sure she really understands what is involved in her decision and why would she be willing to make such a sacrifice for an old man she hardly even knew. Part of the regimen required us meeting together with a member of the transplant team to probe even deeper, seeking to discover her motive for her act of kindness. This team member was not Mr. Personality and it was evident that he had his suspicions about her decision. Looking at me he asked what had I promised to elicit such generosity on her behalf. Not totally satisfied with my reply to his questions, he turned to Ashley.
"Has Mr. Britt offered you anything to prompt you to give him one of your kidneys - an automobile or house?"
Again, Ashley shared her testimony how God alone had impressed her that this was His will for her life and mine. With what seemed to be some skepticism the meeting was concluded.

Fortunately, the Kidney Foundation covered all the expenses for her hospital stay and for the surgery that was to follow. In the following months, Carolyn and I spent a large amount of time getting to know this lovely young lady that was to literally save my life and make it possible for me to continue to preach His Word and serve Him.

GOD'S DELAYS ARE NOT HIS DENIALS

Finally, the closing days of May came and Ashley and I entered the hospital late in the afternoon. Some final testing was done and Carolyn and I anxiously awaited the surgery that was to begin at five o'clock the next morning. Someone knocked at the door and Dr. Mark Deierhoi (pronounced deer hoy), the head of the Transplant Department and the person that was to perform my surgery, entered the room. Taking a seat, he said, "Mr. Britt, I have got some good news and some bad news. The good news is you are going to get a kidney, the bad news is, not tomorrow." He went on to explain that in the very last blood work, some antibodies were discovered. They were present because of the gall bladder surgery and the blood transfusion experienced at that time. The antibodies would definitely result in rejection of the new kidney. We conversed for a brief period and he left the room and Carolyn and I had a few moments of tears, but there was also a peace that flooded my heart and soul. Immediately Psalms 31:15 came to mind, "my times are in your hand," and Psalms 37:23, "the steps of a good man are ordered by the Lord."

Without a doubt, my only goodness is that imputed to me by the Grace of God, when he put me in Christ, but those two truths settled my heart. I now wept for Ashley. A number of friends and her mother had traveled from Mississippi for the operation, and now they were to return home with disappointment. Carolyn and I left UAB hospital that night with sadness, yet with a peace that defied all understanding. I had preached it, now could I live it? His delays are not His denials. It was a new opportunity for our faith to be tested and stretched.

THE DONOR'S DOUBTS

Unbeknown to me, Ashley began to be besieged by her own doubts. I have never known a person more intense in seeking God's will for her life. Because of this postponement of surgery, some of her friends felt that this delay was God's way of telling her that she had been released from her commitment. It was suggested that she, like Abraham, had been willing to make this tremendous sacrifice, but now that the Lord had seen her total obedience, she was released from her pledge. This was a real test to her decision.

Another dilemma arose because of a lack of communication, a problem for which I take full responsibility. The physicians at UAB made the decision that we should set the date for the transplant the following January. I assumed too much when I presumed that they had also contacted Ashley concerning this new date. She felt that she should have been included in this decision, and rightly so. I was totally unaware that she was having these struggles until after the surgery.

Each time I visited the clinic for post operative tests and meeting with the transplant surgeons, I am handed a thick volume that begins with our first contact with the hospital. It is a detailed chronology of every phone call, every test result, and every item concerning my condition and her record and contacts she had made with the hospital. One day, many weeks after the operation, I was thumbing through the volume and read a brief note as to how she had voiced some doubt about her commitment. My blood ran cold when I discovered how close she came to backing out, and how insensitive I had been in assuming too much. But because of Ashley's walk with the Lord, she sought His face and followed through like the trooper she was and is.

The months passed slowly by as we anticipated the first week of January 2001. I remained the interim pastor at Palmerdale Baptist. My physical condition worsened, I became weaker, congestive heart failure became an issue at times, and worst of all, I had to return to the dialysis center for treatment three times a week. Home dialysis was not clearing my body of toxins, as it should. The head nurse at the center brought cheer to my life in those days before surgery by telling me I would never get a transplant because of my weakened condition. Just what I needed.

CHAPTER 30

THE DAY OF DELIVERANCE

I am completely verbally bankrupt in seeking to express the joy of my soul as I entered UAB hospital on January second. Because of total exhaustion, I made my entrance by way of a wheelchair. While Carolyn and I filled out the needed papers for admission, nurses and employees came to greet me with tears. Ashley had already arrived and shared her testimony of how God had led her to make this sacrifice. As those people greeted me, they told how they had never heard such a story and some of them just praised the Lord.

It was late in the afternoon and I was taken to an area for my very last dialysis and then to my room. The doctor entered the room and announced that everything was a go. That night was one of sleeplessness, not because of dread, but out of the sheer excitement of the following morning. Ashley's mother, a Godly lady, came by with a promise of God she found in the Book and had prayer with us.

It is five o'clock in the morning and I am wheeled to the pre operation area. Ashley's gurney is right next to mine. As we converse, the nurses arrive to prepare us for surgery. They insert the IV into my wrist and as they begin to probe for a vein for Ashley, they try again and again before they finally succeed. I watch as the tears make their way down her face, but not a word of complaint. I weep as I consider her total willingness to meet my need. Again, what a soldier, what a trooper. Thank you Lord Jesus!

She goes in one direction for the removal of her kidney and I am wheeled into the surgery room for a few words with attending physicians and nurses. It is a strange experience to so excitedly look forward to the administering of the anesthesia and to welcome the scalpel. As is always the case though, the procedure takes a number of hours. I awaken with the question, "Is it over?"

To me it seemed no more than the blinking of the eye. I am greeted with the words of the success of the operation, but also that the kidney was making urine before all the stitches were in place.

THE PROVIDENCE OF GOD

Affirmation after affirmation gave evidence to the will and providence of God. I was not aware that Ashley went to the hospital days before the surgery and insisted that she be permitted to donate her own blood in case it was needed. She was told that it was not necessary because the need for blood had not occurred in other donor surgeries. She could not be dissuaded and at her insistence her blood was taken and kept in case of any emergency. During her operation the surgeons called for a transfusion and her blood was available. Had she not been so sensitive to the Lord's leadership, any transfusion of another person's blood would have concluded the transplant surgery.

TASTE BUD REVIVAL

There is something about dialysis that makes all food almost tasteless. Whether it is a filet mignon or a hot dog it is almost like eating cardboard. One day after surgery and the food tray is delivered to my room. I take the first bite of meat, and oh, boy, what a delight. There is absolutely no exaggeration when I tell you that not one single grain of rice, not one solitary kernel of corn, not a crumb of bread or speck of meat remains on my plate. For the first time in five years, I can honestly say, that was one of the best meals I had ever eaten. Snacks were delivered to the room each evening and I looked forward to the rap on my door and the succulent tidbits placed on my table. One downside, healed taste buds are not good for the waistline.

DAYS OF RECUPERATION

Two days after surgery, Ashley dropped by the room to say goodbye as she heads back to Mississippi to regain her strength. She is willing to show us the incision where they had to break a rib and remove the lifesaving kidney. I weep as I again try to offer adequate words of appreciation, but my vocabulary is too impoverished.

After two weeks I am released from the hospital. The functioning of the new kidney must be closely monitored to make sure there are no signs of rejection. This required rising before daylight to make our way to the hospital. Carolyn has a real fear of driving on the freeway, so our daily excursion to the clinic took twice as long and I groaned with pain as we encountered every bump and pothole. On arrival at six o'clock we made our way to the lab for blood and urine analysis. We then had to wait for a check of vital signs, followed by a wait to see the pharmacist. Next we had to hang around to see one of the transplant surgeons. The process usually took about six hours, and when a person is experiencing serious discomfort, it seemed like an eternity.

The five days a week became a three times a week, but still it was taking a toll on Carolyn and my condition worsened rather than improving. It was finally discovered that I was having chronic bladder infections, one of which nearly proved fatal, so I was readmitted to the hospital for another two week stay. With heavy doses of antibiotics, I finally began to have a normal recovery for transplant patients.

In about six weeks I was able to return to Palmerdale Baptist to continue serving as interim pastor. They had been so gracious in calling an interim - interim in my absence. Again, I can only praise God for letting me serve such gracious, generous people for three years.

CHAPTER 31

ANOTHER OPEN DOOR

I can identify with Paul when he said, "Woe is me if I preach not the gospel." And Jeremiah when he cried aloud, "His Word in my heart is like a fire, a fire shut up in my bones."

As I have said before, I do not preach to live, but I do live to preach. A call from God to preach defies explanation in seeking to describe the drive that compels the preacher to stand before others and open the Book and share His Word. One must always examine his motives for sure, but the new man in Christ Jesus cries out to exercise the spiritual gift bestowed by God. I seek not to judge others, but I have great difficulty understanding men of God who can retire and still not sense the urgency of preaching His Word. I can think of no greater anguish that comes to a man's soul than when through some moral compromise he disqualifies himself from standing in the pulpit and saying, "Thus saith the Lord." More than I fear cancer or any other catastrophe, I fear becoming what Paul calls 'a cast away.'

It is out of that longing to preach, I share one of the most blessed experiences of my life.

On a Monday, as I drove to attend our local Pastors Conference, I expressed my burden to the Lord. I prayed audibly, but with my eyes open, "Lord, you know the desire of my heart. I have never mailed out a resume in all the years of ministry. You know my address and phone number. I am asking you to open a new door of opportunity."

That very afternoon when I returned home, Carolyn told me of a call from a fellow by the name of Wayne Polk asking me to return his phone call. Having no knowledge of who he was or what he wanted, I returned the call. He informed me that he was a staff member of Cropwell Baptist Church and that their pastor had resigned after more than twenty years of service, and that my name had been submitted as a possible candidate to serve as Interim Pastor. The following day I met with him, some deacons and the pulpit committee. After thorough investigation and questioning, I was invited to preach the following Wednesday night and the next Sunday.

That Wednesday night I experienced something I had never seen in more than fifty years of ministry. Standing before the congregation, I said, "Open your Bibles with me to…." Before I could announce the text, every person stood in unison in honor of His Word. As I moved into the message, every eye was fixed on the preacher, and most of the people took notes of all that was said. The following Sunday, I witnessed the same reverence and I have never preached with such liberty. As I left that Sunday night, I was informed that there were a couple of other preachers they wanted to hear, and they would get in touch with me later. Two weeks went by without a word and I groaned in my spirit. I wanted so badly to be their choice. I must admit that I was afraid they were going to call someone else to serve as interim. Finally the phone rang and I was told that I was invited to preach again the following Sunday and that the church would cast their votes as to whether or not to call me. What a blessing when they called that afternoon to ask me to come as their interim pastor.

Altogether, I have preached in more than a thousand churches, but no fellowship exceeds the kindness, the maturity and spirit of those dear people. I am convinced that the spirituality of that fellowship of believers can be attributed to the former pastor, who faithfully preached expository messages from the Word for more than twenty years. No gimmicks, no pony shows, no bells and whistles, just the Book.

I would to God, that every young pastor would commit himself to that kind of ministry. Carolyn and I had the privilege of serving there more than ten months. I must confess that I was disappointed when they finally called a new pastor. When our last Sunday night was completed, the people gave us a reception fit for a king. Thank you, Lord Jesus, for such an opportunity.

THE SPOILED PREACHER

The only way to explain it is to say, "This preacher got spoiled." Like a little child that only ate dessert for years, perhaps my expectations were too lofty. Cropwell Church was such an oasis, a little taste of heaven; it seemed to Carolyn and me that, perhaps subconsciously, I was seeking another such fellowship. It is with no boast that I say five other churches invited me to come as their interim pastor, but I sensed no definite leadership of the Lord that I should accept any of these invitations. I did recommend two of my preacher friends to fill the pulpit and they were called to serve in an interim capacity. One of the churches even called one of these fellows as full time pastor.

CHAPTER 32

HYPOCHONDRIAC?

Me, suffering from hypochondria? I hope not. If there is anything more boring or aggravating, it is to listen to someone talk about how they are enjoying poor health, unless it is when you are reviewing your ailments and someone is able to top your parade of illnesses. I hate to be around people like that, especially when I am looking for sympathy. But for whatever reason, our Lord has permitted me to walk some dark valleys. However, it is always for my good and His glory.

It was during those days of dialysis that I began to experience neuropathy. Peripheral neuropathy is a slow moving, but progressive disorder that affects the nerve endings of the body's extremities. It is a malady that is most often associated with diabetics, but thankfully, that is one problem I have not encountered. First, I began to notice numbness of my toes and then my feet and my lower legs. And now it has progressed above my knees. Perhaps, the most aggravating aspect of the ailment is losing feeling in my fingers and hands. Walking and balance has become difficult and turning the pages of the newspaper or a book can be maddening. Trying to tie a fishing plug onto monofilament line will make you want to scream. Attempting to fasten the collar button will drive you nuts, though that is a short distance for me.

I am sure that pride is the root problem that causes me to be self conscious about having to have aide to ascend and descend to the platform to preach. I am constantly discovering that it is much easier to preach about, "giving thanks for all things," than it is to practice it.

GROWING OLD IS NOT FOR SISSIES

There is a purpose in listing this litany of sob stories other than to gain much needed sympathy. They all relate to the ministry He has called me to.

I have related earlier the account of the problem with my vision and the Lord's gracious intervention to let me keep my sight in my right eye. After the lens implant during cataract surgery, I am blessed to have 20/15 eyesight, but in time driving at night increasingly became a problem. Facing oncoming traffic and bright street lights was all but blinding. Trying to drive on a rainy night became frightening. This was another bitter pill to swallow and difficult to admit and accept.

Hillview Baptist Church, a fellowship across the city, extended a call for me to serve as their Interim Pastor. It was with real excitement that we accepted the invitation. Here was another opportunity to exercise the gift the Lord had bestowed upon me. Again, the Father permitted us a place to serve where the people were kind, generous and gracious. For the first and only time in my life, I had to inform the deacons that the honorarium was too generous and the remuneration was reduced. The dilemma of poor night vision became a real problem and after a few months I was forced to resign and recommend a fellow preacher.

BACK TO GLORY LAND

In June of 2007, Carolyn and I went to our lake house after church on Sunday. We were eating at the Steak House in Pell City when some members of Cropwell Baptist Church began to enter the restaurant. Kind friends from that fellowship came to our table and informed us that their pastor had just resigned after serving for five years. Several stated that they had already suggested that the Pulpit Committee should contact us to return as their Interim. Our hearts leaped with joy as to the opportunity and God's perfect timing. In a matter of days, the call came, asking us to return to the sweetest fellowship this side of heaven. God is so good, all the time.

One good thing about accepting this call was that the highway to the church was marked with bright reflectors on the center lane and easy to see lines on the road's edge, so for the next ten months we were privileged to minister to this wonderful fellowship again.

I am sure that when one only ministers on Sundays and Wednesday nights, he is oblivious to the common gripes and groans of the congregation, but that has its blessings. One would have to visit Cropwell to find that I am not exaggerating when I commend the people there. Sunday after Sunday, the music was indeed a blessing. There was such enthusiasm in the worship services and the people offered their appreciation for the messages, often with tears in their eyes. People were saved, numbers came to join the church and a taste of revival was experienced.

Just one example of their kindness and thoughtfulness was revealed one Sunday morning. Because of my lack of balance, it was necessary for me to be assisted to the platform each service. At the conclusion of the message, I had to have aide to leave the platform to receive people during the invitation. But, bless the Lord, after about two weeks of watching the decrepit old man ascend the steps to preach, I walked into the auditorium to see two beautiful, ornamental railings leading up to the platform. What a fellowship, what a joy divine!

Again, our gracious God permitted us to remain with these dear people for almost a year and then they called a new pastor. Among the many compliments bestowed by the people, none was more cherished than when many leaders said, "Brother Bobby, you met a great need at the time we needed it the most." Perhaps they over stated the issue, but I can tell you that they met a need in my life when I needed it the most.

CHAPTER 33

STILL WATERS DISTURBED

During those days at Cropwell, I often spoke of how God was allowing Carolyn and me to enjoy calm and placid seas. I knew from experience and the Word that at any time a fresh storm could arise and our days of tranquility could be disrupted. In fact, I expected times of testing to be part of our future. It was not an attitude of negativity, but of reality. I imagined that any new trial could not be as difficult as those experienced in past days, but the deepest valley yet loomed on the horizon.

For a number of months Carolyn experienced increasing weakness, nausea and loss of appetite. Although she was under the care of a physician whose reputation was impeccable, her conditioned worsened. One night she discovered a swelling in her lower right abdomen. Upon the next visit to the doctor, she told him of her discovery and as he examined her he recommended an immediate cat scan and it was determined that she had a large tumor attached to the ovary. Some days later an oncologist estimated the tumor to weigh as much as twenty-five pounds and that surgery should be scheduled as soon as possible.

Storm clouds again appeared and the calm, tranquil sea began to swell and white capped waves were discomforting as they pounded our little vessel.

DAYS BECOME WEEKS

Now under the care of a reputable oncologist, surgery is scheduled for July 1, 2008. We are admitted into Trinity

Medical Center with the assurance that Carolyn will have a five to seven day hospital stay and a six to eight week time of recovery. The entire family and a host of friends wait anxiously for the surgeon to emerge and give us a good report of a very successful procedure. A nurse calls us into a family room to tell us that due to the size of the tumor, the procedure will take longer than expected. After more than five hours Dr. Maxwell enters the waiting room, takes the family aside to give us the report. The tumor weighed more than ten pounds and not only had it attached to other organs, but it was malignant. He felt that all the cancer had been localized and removed, but in the process of lifting the tumor, the ureter, the tube from the kidney to the bladder, had been torn. He assured us that he had stitched the ureter and things looked good, assuring us that she would be dismissed in about a week.

I could not restrain myself from weeping when I heard the word 'cancer.' Carolyn's mother and two of her aunts had died because of the menacing and merciless malady. It was with dread that I considered seeing her in the recovery room and pondered how in this world could I honestly reveal the doctor's finding? It was a relief when a young and bright associate of the surgeon ventured to report their findings as we all gathered about her bed. I was amazed at Carolyn's faith and courage as she received the word and we agreed to face this new time of testing with faith in our Living and Loving Lord. I cannot imagine what it is to be an unbeliever and receive the unspeakable news of such a dark valley.

HORRENDOUS HAPPENINGS

In the days immediately following surgery, Carolyn did not improve, but her conditioned worsened markedly. Her body began to bloat and swell. She could not and would not eat. During the first night she vomited a black noxious fluid and the physicians had no ready answers. Because I feared she might strangle, unable to have immediate assistance from the nurses, I determined to stay with her night and day. I had been involved in a head on collision in a friend's pick up three days before her surgery that resulted in severe back pain. Attempting to sleep in a recliner in her room dealt me misery. Thank God for sweet daughters-in-law who gave me some relief as they offered to spend the night with her.

That five to seven day hospital stay finally resulted into a seventy-seven day period of agony, anguish and misery. It is one thing to find the sufficiency of God's grace in my own personal trials, but it is far different when seeing your mate, the one you love, weeping in pain and experiencing worsening conditions day after day and night after night. In a matter of weeks, the situation began to take a toll on me. I found myself experiencing depression and often sobbing out my grief when I would drive away from the hospital and when I returned home. Without self-pity, I became concerned about my own mental, emotional and physical condition. Some friends and family did offer some relief on different occasions, especially Carolyn's cousin, Linda, but I knew that Carolyn wanted me to be with her, and that was also my desire.

GOOD SAMARITANS

E-mail is a wonderful invention. Because of the Lord's blessing in letting me travel from coast to coast and border to border in evangelism, He has given me brothers and sisters all over the country. I would contact friends almost every day, giving them the latest report of Carolyn's condition. From Africa to California, from the tip of Florida to the Canadian Border, friends by the hundreds were interceding for her and for me. In one such e-mail, I asked that they would pray for me to be strengthened to properly care for Carolyn. Shortly after that request I received a call from Cropwell Baptist Church, informing me that they were asking their people to sign a list and offer their services to sit with Carolyn and give me some relief. Soon they were daily arriving, two by two, to spend the morning hours at her side. Although I only missed going to the hospital three days of the seventy-seven of her confinement, I was able to sleep late and even find time for recreation in the morning hours. Such sacrifice, such love, only to be found in the family of God.

A SPECIAL SACRIFICE

A member of that sweet fellowship offered a special ministry, one that was above the call of duty. Brother Terry Moore had a service that provided sitters for the homebound and for those in the hospital that needed special attention. His agency was called "Waiting Angels," and that they were. He called me one day and offered to provide someone to stay with Carolyn each and every night, and at no cost. The nights I did not stay with her, I was paying individuals $100 each night to take my place. I could only weep and praise God for such kindness and sacrificial generosity provided by the saints of God. Hey, it pays to serve Jesus, every day and in every way.

GROANINGS THAT CANNOT BE UTTERED

It has been said that it is not too difficult to forgive those who hurt you, but it is more problematic to forgive those who hurt those you love. Likened unto that statement, I would add that it is not too difficult to deal with one's own personal testings, but it is far tougher to deal with the physical sufferings and agony of the one you love the most. It seemed that everything that could go wrong did go wrong. Not one physician could offer any diagnosis that made sense or logic. All they could do was surmise as to her worsening condition. It became evident that she was literally fighting for her very life. Her body became so bloated that large blisters began to develop on her legs and feet. When therapists would come to aide her as she attempted to walk down the hall, I would follow and wipe the floor as fluid seeped through the pores of her flesh.

The most agonizing day arrived when a renal specialist came to her room and informed Carolyn that dialysis was a necessity if she was to live. We both shuddered at the suggestion because she had witnessed the difficulty we faced during my five year stint with the treatments after my kidney failure. We both unashamedly wept at the very thought of the three days a week to be spent at a dialysis center. To compound the treatments, the nurses, in that particular area, seemed to be without compassion or sympathy. On one particular day, the renal physician chose to use words of vulgarity while Carolyn was being dialyzed. She returned to her room to inform me she would not have another treatment because of the rudeness and offensiveness of the doctor. Explaining the details of the incident, I bristled with righteous indignation. I called the Office of Administration to voice my complaint and demanded to have a consultation with the jerk. A few minutes passed and the telephone rang and the quack began to explain his reason for his inappropriate language. In my anger, I interrupted him to inform him that I was Christian and a minister, but that I was also a man, and if that incident was ever repeated he would have me to deal with me. Oddly enough, he never came to Carolyn's room again, but sent his associate. Hey, say and do what you will to me, but don't mess with my wife or my boys.

CHAPTER 34

PEACE IN THE MIDST OF THE STORM

Although a number of friends and some family members felt that Carolyn would not live, the Lord continued to give me assurance that He would sustain her life, but it did appear she would spend the rest of her life on dialysis and would probably have a colostomy. Day by day, He would give me a word through His Word. I would share those promises with her. More than two months had now passed and her condition continued to deteriorate. She was now under the care of an oncologist, a nutritionist, renal specialists, a physician that dealt only with blood diseases, and even had a visit from a psychiatrist. None had any answers. I discovered that doctors are a lot like preachers; it is difficult, if not impossible, for either to simply say, "I don't know." Too often, both categories of men suffer from a Messiah complex.

MISERABLE BIRTHDAY

It is now August 31st, sixty-one days since her surgery. Very few times of laughter or moments of pleasure have brought a smile to her lovely face. The visits from our sons and daughters-in-law and the grandchildren resulted in momentary levity. The only times of real enjoyment were those days when she felt able to let me roll her in a wheelchair outside the hospital to breathe the fresh air and see the blue sky, to hear the sweet sound of a chirping bird and relish the beauty of flowers in the court yard. August 31st was a special day. It was her seventy-first birthday. I contacted the family and asked them to help me surprise her with a special celebration. Hospital personnel agreed to let us decorate one end of the cafeteria. A huge cake with candles was prepared, refreshments galore lined the tables and a number of friends and all the family gathered for the occasion. Now, how do I get a sick wife down to the place of celebration? By telling a lie, of course. I told her there were friends downstairs that could not physically come to her room, and would be disappointed if she could not see them. Reluctantly she let me wheel her down to the first floor, into the cafeteria and into the presence of about thirty combined voices singing 'Happy Birthday.' Like any normal woman, she was embarrassed because of no makeup and her hair was somewhat disheveled. To top it off, she felt terrible and could only remain for a few minutes. Returning to her room, terrific nausea gripped her swollen body and the rest of the night was spent in misery. 'Happy Birthday'? No, it was a miserable birthday, one that will never be forgotten.

A WORD FROM THE LORD

Romans 10:17 says that 'faith comes by hearing and hearing by the word of God.' The word used here by Paul for 'word' is *rhema* and carries with it the idea of a special utterance or a specific word to the individual. This came to have special meaning early one morning while I was having my quiet time reading in the Book of Genesis. In the eighth chapter and the first verse it says, "And God remembered Noah...." Surely Noah had not been absent from the mind of God, but God remembered him in a special way. Though it was not an audible voice I heard that morning, God spoke to my heart and said, "Son, I am remembering you and Carolyn today."

My heart leapt with joy, tears brimmed my eyes, and I could hardly wait to get to the hospital that morning and share God's word to me that day. That day the doctor ordered another cat scan of Carolyn's swollen, distorted abdomen. We prayed that our Lord would give some new revelation of her problem that very day. The procedure revealed a massive amount of fluid surrounding her stomach and immediately a drain was inserted in her abdomen, and within a brief amount of time five liters of black, odorous urine were expelled from that area. It was finally determined that the ureter, the tube from the kidney to the bladder, had come unstitched and urine had been deposited in the abdomen for weeks. Praise God, the source of her ailment was discovered and from that very moment she began to show marked improvement.

In the midst of the joy and praising God for the beginning of the healing process, I harbored anger in my heart, knowing that someone had failed to properly diagnose the source of her near fatal illness. I pondered the weeks of needless physical and emotional agony she had experienced and thoughts of a lawsuit often came to mind. I was disappointed that not one physician would fault any colleague nor assume any responsibility for a misdiagnosis.

BRIEF MOMENTS OF REFRESHING

As Carolyn and I look back on those days of hospital confinement, very few moments of real joy come to mind. Certainly there was a deep appreciation for those who came to visit, for those who really aided in times of desperate need. The times most cherished are those of our children and grandchildren standing and sitting about the room. But, most of the time it was almost a forced laughter that would occasionally erupt from her aching body. The most memorable occasions were those times when she finally became strong enough for me to place her in a wheelchair and take her outside the four confining walls of her room. As we would find our little spot on the sidewalk, next to the hospital entrance, tears would brim our eyes as she relished the sound of a chirping sparrow, as she expressed such deep gratitude to just be able to take deep breaths of the fresh air. Some days when she felt strong enough, we would venture across the street to a small courtyard and take pleasure in the beauty of the blooming pansies and marigolds. Funny how the little things that are often unnoticed and unappreciated become so very important when one's life is almost hanging by a thread and that which is simple becomes precious.

RELEASED FROM PRISON

Monday, September 17, 2008, a day that Carolyn will never forget. Etched in her memory as that day she was released from her imprisonment. It was now dark when the papers were properly signed and we exited the hospital. I had arranged for a three by seven foot banner be placed across the garage door. It read, 'WELCOME HOME CAROLYN.' All the neighbors in our garden home community had been alerted as well as family members, and as we turned into the driveway they applauded her arrival. It was a halleluiah day for me and for her. Home at last, home at last. Praise God!

A SHORT LIVED JOY

Since 1971 we have been privileged to own a lake house on the Coosa River, located about forty-five minutes from our home. Because of Carolyn's confinement, I felt it would be good for us to venture to the lake, sit out on the porch, and enjoy the sunshine and nature. Bad decision. We spent one night and the next day she awoke with a critically high fever and became extremely ill. She refused to let me call her doctor, fearing another hospital stay. By that afternoon she became much worse and her fever elevated. Calling the doctor, he urgently demanded that I get her to the hospital immediately. With some difficulty we got her into the car and made a beeline to Trinity. She was now desperately ill and I drove ninety to one hundred miles an hour to the emergency room. It was discovered she had a lingering blood infection that could have been fatal. It was with great frustration she endured another ten day hospitalization.

Let me close this sad saga by saying that she had to return to the hospital on two more occasions in the weeks to come. Because of her weakened condition, she could not have surgery to correct the detached ureter and I had to learn to be the home bound nurse. IVs were a necessity three or four times a day. A tube had been inserted through her back to the kidney for urination, nutrients and vitamins had to be carefully combined and fed through the IV, incisions had to be medicated, cleansed and bandaged daily, and in short order I felt I deserved a nurse's degree. It would have been a fine accomplishment since I never had earned a Doctorate. These were difficult days indeed, but they brought about a deeper love and appreciation for one another and gave me an opportunity to try and meet her needs as she had so willingly met mine during the past days of kidney failure, five years of dialysis and the kidney transplant.

CHAPTER 35

WHOM THE LORD LOVES HE DISCIPLINES

With tongue in cheek, I sometimes want to say, "Lord, I wish you didn't love me so much," but not really. Just before my kidney transplant, word of Ashley Fisher's gracious sacrifice to become my donor circulated throughout the community and even the entire state. Our Denominational paper, The Alabama Baptist, ran an article on the seemingly miraculous intervention of God in making the transplant possible. A little later, a writer for the Birmingham News asked permission to come to our home and interview me and write an article about the experience. The writer was a kind individual with a very positive confession of his faith in the Lord Jesus and his personal salvation. In essence, he asked me to share the personal experiences of my life up till the present moment. As I related some of the valleys God had seen me through, he laid aside his pencil and with teary eyes he asked, "Brother Bobby, why is it God allows so many things to come to some individuals?" And then he added, "I have never had such trials in my Christian experience." I pondered his inquiry for a few moments, prayed silently, asking that He would give me wisdom to properly answer his probing question. I replied, "Wayne, there are some people who are more strong willed and hard headed than others, and a loving God is seeking to break the stubborn will of that individual in order to make him a more useful vessel. I also am convinced that our Lord has a special ministry for each of His children and He knows exactly how to prepare each person for that unique ministry. He says that we are to "comfort others with the same comfort whereby we have been comforted by Him." I closed our conversation with what I am sure were unsettling words. "Wayne, although you have never been through dark valleys in your Christian experience, those days will come, you can be sure."

Not many months had passed until he and his sweet wife learned that she had a very aggressive cancer and in due time, the Lord called her home. Wayne, though broken hearted, bore and still bears a vibrant testimony of the sufficient Grace of God.

I mention this experience with the hope that the rehearsals of the testing times our Lord has permitted in my personal life will not appear as the musings of a hypochondriac. They are as sure to come to every child of God as tomorrow's sunrise. And when the writer of the Book of Hebrews tells us that, "whom the Lord loves He chastens." Surely there is the legitimate application of that twelfth chapter that makes it clear that when a child of God rebels and gets out of His will, the Lord will not spare the rod. But, of greater application is to realize that as a loving Father, He disciplines us to mold us into the image of His Son.

What relief and peace will come to the heart of the born again person when he or she realizes that at the moment of conversion, our Lord places that individual on the Potter's Wheel and slowly and gradually begins the process of molding that child into a vessel, not only fit for a unique service, but one who is made like unto the Person of the Lord Jesus. The only time that vessel is taking shape is when the Potter's hand is exerting pressure on the clay and the process in the kiln is uncomfortable indeed, but the finished product will reveal the Divine creativity of the Potter.

WHAT'S IT ALL ABOUT?

One of the most treasured privileges of almost sixty years of ministry is that of the individuals our Lord has brought into my life. In pages to come I will list some of those individuals whom God has used to influence, challenge and mold my life. Of those persons, no one is more treasured than my friend, Ron Dunn. I met Ron during seminary days at Southwestern in Ft. Worth, Texas. On my last occasion to fellowship with Ron, he was in Birmingham at a local church. As he and I rehearsed fond memories of classes and professors, mutual friends, some who had gone to be with the Lord, and revival meetings I had been privileged to preach in churches he had served as Pastor, he paused and made what would have been a humbling statement had it not been true. With a twinkle in his black as coal eyes and a smile on his face he said, "And, Britt, back then, we didn't have a clue as to what it was all about."

Now that would seem to be a real putdown to a fellow that had preached almost eight hundred revivals, had seen many, many folks saved, had served as a pastor for more than a dozen years, but I knew in reality, he had spoken the truth. In my zeal for the Lord, I had focused on ministry, on how many souls had been saved, on being a faithful servant of the Savior. But finally God had finally revealed to me that, 'what it's all about', is the *Glory of God*. Don't casually read those words, 'The Glory of God', and dismiss what I attempt to share.

THE GLORY OF GOD

Just what is the 'Glory of God'? Someone has defined the Glory of God as all that God does and all that He is. Ponder that explanation long and hard. The greatest revelation of all that God is and does was exhibited in the Person and life of His Son and our Savior, the Lord Jesus. And that is what it is all about, His being now, presently, revealed in and through us. It is not about buildings and baptisms, so called success or position. When a person can come to focus on His being made manifest, then one can 'count it all joy' and 'in everything give thanks' and 'give thanks for all things.' That does not mean that we don't hurt and weep, but it does mean that when difficult days come, we can know that He intends to use our deepest sufferings to mold us into His image and to reveal Himself, His Glory, to a world that desperately needs to see Him in all of His fullness.

CHAPTER 36

A DIFFERENT MINISTRY

Because of Carolyn's lengthy hospital stay and the months of convalescence upon returning home, I declined every speaking engagement. I did so because of need, but mainly out of desire. She was so weak; she was unable to even lift herself out of a chair. Her Doctor, who specialized in nutrition, was seriously concerned about her diet. Severe malnutrition had occurred in her extended hospitalization and it was only with our insistence he signed her release. Assuring him that I am a pretty good chef, he gave me instructions as to the high protein foods that must be prepared daily. Only problem, she would not cooperate in eating. I found that the ministry, now committed to me, was that of a caregiver. Somehow, females just seem more accomplished at this than men. Because of her difficult recovery and my sometimes lack of patience, we did have our brief times of less than friendly exchange, but seeing her suffer as she had, knowing that she was often near death, recalling how she had cared for me in my times of illness, there developed a deeper love for one another than any we had ever known. I would not recommend this method for making a good marriage even better, but in finality, it has been worth it all.

It has now been more than two years since Carolyn's final repair surgery. She is still declared to be cancer free, and she again is in the 'go mode.' God has given her a real talent for crafts, vintage clothing and she is constantly working with her hands. She maintains a booth in an antique mall and busies herself in maintaining that venture. She has vintage fashion shows several times a year and recently had nearly 200 women in attendance as the models displayed a host of wedding dresses.

One never really appreciates life until the Lord permits that individual to come to the place where you stare the grim reaper in the face and walk away knowing that Jesus has truly removed the sting of death and the black caped fiend no longer holds you in fear or dread. What a Savior!

CHAPTER 37

POSESSING OUR POSESSIONS

In no wise would I equate the difficulties of my life or those of any Christian with Israel's wanderings in the desert. We have already crossed over Jordan through the death, burial and resurrection of the Lord Jesus. Canaan land does not represent heaven, but rather the land of promise where there are still many foes to be conquered and He has equipped us with all that is needed to defeat the enemy. Our desperate need is to daily, and moment by moment, appropriate all that He makes available for the warfare in which we are engaged. Truly, He means for us to be 'more than conquerors.' But again, it is easier said than done, easier to preach than to practice. If one is not very careful, we will become weary in well doing.

Without boasting, I can honestly say that I only lost one fistfight my entire life, and I did not just lose that fight, I got my brains beat out. I was working as a curb hop at the aforementioned 'Polar Bear' or 'Spinning Wheel.' From three to eight teenage guys worked as business demanded. A new guy was hired who soon came to be the boss's favorite. We nicknamed him Brownie for obvious reasons. I can't explain it, but nobody liked him except Maw Dye, the manager of the business. He was not very manly and sometimes seemed quite sissified. Without being able to recall the reason, he and I got into a heated argument. Stupidly, I invited him outside to settle the issue. Just outside the door, I turned to raise my fist, and before I could land one punch, ole' Brownie popped me in the face and I was flat on my back. Scrambling to my feet, I swung and missed and another punch put me on my posterior. Every time I got up he knocked me down. All my buddies just stood around and let him beat the daylights out of me. Finally, a customer got out of his car, helped me to my feet and broke up the embarrassing melee.

I relate that humiliating incident to draw a comparison concerning the gigantic waves of difficulty that God allows to invade our lives. It is one thing to face the occasional trials that come to all of His children, but quite another to seemingly have the whitecaps relentlessly beat upon our little vessels, to feel that one blow after another smacks our feeble frame. Often one is tempted to just hang it up, to try to roll with the punches or just stay down and not get back up. When that occurs, one wallows in the slough of despair, depression soon follows, and one long pity party becomes a quagmire of failure. I know because I have been there. Our Lord is in no way honored or glorified, and the victim becomes the focus of his own attention and the attention of all those who surround him. Then we must remember the Word of the Lord found in Hebrews 12:12 that reminds us: *Wherefore lift up the hands which hang down, and the feeble knees.*

HEROES OF THE FAITH

The longer our Lord allows me to live and preach His Word, the deeper my appreciation, respect and admiration grows for some select saints of God. I speak of those individuals whose lives reveal genuine, biblical endurance, that is, to bear up under trouble, stress, and heavy burdens for lengthy seasons. I am now reminded of a wife and mother who gave birth to a special needs child. The husband, father of the daughter, flew the coop, so to speak, because the demands upon his lifestyle were too uncomfortable, too challenging, so he walked away from the marriage. That mother has cared for that child, now an adult, almost without complaint, forgiving and holding no bitterness.

A husband comes to mind, a kind and gentle man, who married a lady who was the mother of a severely retarded son. Her husband had also left her, because he was unwilling to make the sacrifices that would be necessary to raise the afflicted child. I observed the couple as they brought that teenage son to church, and with tears of admiration, I witnessed the loving concern this man revealed as he sat by that boy Sunday after Sunday, and almost every Wednesday night. Always a smile, never a word of complaint, just revealing the love of God and bearing the fruit of the Spirit, patience, and the ability to bear up under extreme difficulty.

Neither time nor space would allow me to parade the dozens upon dozens of individuals I have met through the years, persons who have borne up under crushing circumstances, people that would be embarrassed to be mentioned by name, heroes of faith in my estimation, who will be richly rewarded at the Judgment Seat of Christ.

Not a few preachers will be asked to step aside as multitudes of these sacred saints are blessed by the words of our Lord and Savior, "Well done, good and faithful servant, you have been faithful in a few things, I will make you ruler over many things."

Truly these are the salt of the earth, God bless them.

TAKEN BY SURPRISE

I am still learning to not boast about the so called *'things I have learned.'* Just when I assumed I have learned, that assumption proves to be obsolete and surely incomplete. God is constantly testing our faith to let us see if it is genuine and stretching that faith to prepare it for future battles and engagements.

It is September 2009, and Carolyn's physical condition is the best in several years. We are making plans for future travel. Consideration is given to fly to Salt Lake, rent a car and visit Yosemite and the Grand Canyon, taking our sweet time with no definite schedule, just go and stay until we get homesick.

But then, some symptoms of a serious nature begin and after a couple of trips to the emergency room, further testing is advised. The examinations reveal a bladder tumor and a biopsy proves it to be a very aggressive type cancer. I am stunned, but not shocked, by the diagnosis. Again, there is a sweet peace that floods my soul as the doctor outlines my options. He recommends that the surgery should be performed as soon as possible, but advises me to return to University Hospital so that my kidney transplant surgeon will be available to assist the urologist who will perform the operation. Following several more procedures, surgery is scheduled for October 16, 2009.

MAKING PLANS FOR GLORY

I can honestly identify with the heart of the Apostle Paul when he says, "I have a desire to depart and be with the Lord, which is far better."

I am not beset by any death wish, but in reality, I can truthfully say that I am sick of this old world. I am weary of its values, its music, the politics, the entertainment and its general rejection and animosity toward our God. Death by cancer or surgical complications that might prove fatal hold no bogey dread on me. I don't mean to sound like a grumpy old man, a malcontent or one who is sour on life, but I look forward to going to see my Savior face to face and dwelling with the saints of the ages and fellowshipping with passed-on family members. (Glory, hold my mule while I shout!) There is the dread of lingering illness that includes suffering and pain for my family, but the only apprehension I experienced was the realization of an extended recovery time following the surgical procedure.

The night before admission to the hospital, I calmly sat down with Carolyn and apprised her of our finances and wrote out my funeral service. Does that sound morbid? I hope not. I got excited about the hymns I would request and the brilliant eulogy that would extol my virtues, Ha, Ha! The following morning as I was prepared for surgery and family members stood about the gurney, I had a peace of God that is without description. Mine was to be a win-win outcome, regardless, healing or heaven. I could not lose!

UNHOLY TERROR

On at least eight occasions I have been placed under general anesthesia. Each time I can remember awaking with the same question, "Is it over?" The time lapse always seemed to be no more that the blinking of an eye. This trip into 'La La Land' was to prove to be far different. For personal reasons, I write of this experience with some reluctance, yet, I feel that it is important.

From my gurney in the pre-surgery room, I bid goodbye to friends and family members. Carolyn follows me to the swinging doors of the surgical suite and gives me a parting kiss. The nurses and physicians scurry about the ice-cold room and inform me as to what is to follow. I joke with the anesthesiologist as he instructs me about the deep breaths that will put me in the 'don't care zone'. Zap, I am gone! My expectations of awakening in a few moments with that usual query, 'Is it over?' fails to materialize. I am hearing voices giving staccato type instructions, and those words addressed to me are expressions of rebuke. Still under the effects of more than eight hours of anesthesia, I try to respond and voice my discomfort, but realize tubes down my throat prevent any complaint or cry for help. Unable to fully realize the situation, I struggle and fight against the restraints that bind my hands and feet to the bed. But most horrifying of all is a terrible sensation of the total abandonment and absence of God. Even in my subconscious condition I was desperately crying out to Him for His aide and comfort, and yet, He was nowhere to be found. I am not sure how long this agony prolonged, but I assure you it was the most horrific, terror filled occurrence of my life. In days to follow, God assured me that my experience was psychological and emotional, induced by mind-boggling anesthesia, but even that reassurance did not and has not removed the dreadfulness of that experience. It was days before I even dared to share with anyone that trip down hell's alley, and for the first time it was revealed to me, at least in part, the awfulness of being lost, cast into Hell and be abandoned by God. I wept afresh as I rehearsed those words of our Savior when He cried, "My God, My God, why hast Thou forsaken me?" Oh, the agony of the soul, "Lord, help me never to forget!"

THAT WHICH I FEARED THE MOST

You know the routine. You are informed that your insurance instructs you that your time in that facility has expired and it is now determined that your uncomfortable hospital bed must be vacated and the luscious meals will no longer be brought to your bedside. But, I am almost too weak to even stand much less walk. All of my doctors insist that I desperately need physical therapy and the only places that are available and covered by my insurance are nursing homes. A chill runs through my frame at the very mention of 'nursing home.' Like Job, I felt "that which I have feared the most has come to pass."

I guess every pastor knows the dread of walking the halls of those facilities, seeing individuals in fetal positions, hearing the constant moaning of poor creatures who have lost all touch with reality, observing the forlorn expressions of patients waiting for the day of ongoing. I realize that I paint, perhaps, a picture far too bleak and dreary, but it has been my experience to meet few folks rejoicing in the Lord in these places, surely some, but they are in the minority.

With all this said, I realized that I was in no condition to return to our little garden home residence and too frail and fragile for Carolyn to manage, so with begrudging reluctance, I agreed to be admitted to such an abode in our vicinity, no more than twenty minutes from our residence.

Upon being wheeled into the building, I was informed that there were only semi-private rooms available. As my brother pushed my wheel chair down the long hallway to my room, my reservations increased the more. Being totally exhausted from the issues of the day, my only desire was to find the bed, crawl up and go to sleep. But, of course, there are a plethora of forms to be filled out, instructions to be given, medications to be listed, etc., etc. Just let me go to bed is my plea and then I see my mattress that looked like it was designed in a banana factory, modeled after a sway backed horse or put through the misery of a four hundred pound woman sitting in one position for a decade.

Finally, some three hours later the lights go out in my little semi-private room and I realize my roommate enjoys turning down the volume, but leaving the television on all night long. After words of pleading persuasion, he turns off the boob tube and commences to snore, grunt and groan and cough till daylight. It is not bad, it is worse than I could have ever expected. Not long after Ole' Sol lifts its head above the horizon, I am on the phone telling, not asking, Carolyn to come and rescue her loving husband.

ONE MORE VALIANT EFFORT

After awhile, Carolyn arrives to what I thought would be my rescue from bedlam, but no, she and others have better plans. She comes to my room accompanied by the head nurse and the superintendent of the facility. They strongly advise me to stay put, telling me it is for my benefit. Inquiring as to my dissatisfaction, assurance is given that changes will be made. They promise a new hospital bed with a new mattress to replace the torture crib that I had cursed, not literally, through the hours of the night. Concerning my snoring, grunting, groaning roommate, he would be sedated to the point of unconsciousness, but please stay a few more days, they pled. Even my oldest son joined in the conspiracy to drive the old man mad. Against all better judgment I succumbed to their pleading. I would give it the old school try and I really meant it. I realized I needed physical rehab because I could hardly stand, much less walk, and I did not want to put more stress and strain on Carolyn. Her words of pleading to let her come home from her three month hospital stay still rang in my ears and I recalled telling her that I was physically unable to give the adequate care she needed. With tears, and sometimes anger and frustration, she felt I wanted her to remain hospitalized rather than face the responsibilities incurred by her release. I thought of ole Pharaoh, when the land was covered with frogs, rather than obey God and release the Israelites he chose 'one more night with the frogs. I, too, chose at least one more night with the 'whatevers.'

SAME SONG, SECOND VERSE

I did get the new bed and mattress, but if they did really try to render my roomie unconscious, they failed miserably. I did request and received enough sedation to finally put me out of my misery for a very few hours of sleep just before daylight. I realized if I was to ever recover and regain my strength, I had to get proper rest and sleep and it sure was not going to happen at my present location. Dialing 655-5860, a sleepy voice answered, "Hello," and with no hesitation, I replied, "Come and get me or I am going to crawl home, but I ain't staying."

To make a long story short, late that afternoon I was finally dismissed amidst smiles on the faces of the nurses, happy to see me leave and a, "Hip, hip, hooray," on my lips as I experienced the emotions of a sparrow released from a rusty cage.

One last thought. That afternoon, one of the kinder nurses came to my bedside and asked, "Mr. Britt, why do you want to go home?" Looking her in the eye I asked,
"When you get off at eleven o'clock tonight and you had the choice of getting into this bed and sleeping or you could go home to your bed, what would you do?" Throwing her head back and laughing out loud, she replied, "I know what you mean and I would head for my house!" "Good bye, Mr. Britt."

HOME AT LAST, THANK GOD, HOME AT LAST

It is early November 2009. Thank God for a loving, caring wife. A few days of wheel chair transportation, graduating to a walker, a walking stick and the old body is pretty much back to normal, whatever that is. Two weeks and two days after surgery, I have the privilege of preaching to our Birmingham Ministers Conference. As I slowly recoup, God is graciously opening doors of preaching opportunities. I am so grateful, for preaching is my life. God willing, I don't want to live many days beyond the ability to share His Word.

Bless the Lord; follow up MRI's reveal no existing cancer cells. Another gracious lease on life.

CHAPTER 38

AND IN CONCLUSION?

In one particular church I pastored, there was a sweet, sweet lady that could talk in conversation for forty-five minutes without taking a breath. All of her dialogue was composed of one single sentence. It seemed she never understood what a question mark, exclamation point or period meant. She was the type person that if she called you on the telephone, you could place the receiver on the desk and go about your business and just give a grunt or a 'yes mam' every so often and she would never know the difference. Of course, you know that I, the pastor, would never do that. What I am trying to say is that she could never seem to come to a conclusion in any conversation.

I think about her as I attempt to come to some sort of termination in putting all these words on paper. In one sense none of us can say, "In conclusion." As I have sought to write these pages, I think of a friend who wrote a volume of his memoirs. I was captivated by the multitude of seeming 'incidentals' included in his autobiography. Discussing that with him, he replied, "Bobby, I don't think there are incidentals in life. They are all important."

Contemplating his wisdom, I am convinced he is on target. In composing this personal memoir, I added so many incidents that on previous evaluation, I considered them unworthy of mention. And in the estimation of many, they might be so deemed. But they have brought laughter and tears in my reflections. So, in conclusion there is really no conclusion. Every day is a new adventure with new lessons to be learned and even at our death there is no ending because our influence for good or bad continues on in the lives of others.

Perhaps you remember the name, Mel Blanc, known as the man of a thousand voices. His was the voice you heard as you watched the cartoons of Elmer Fudd, Porky Pig, Daffy Duck, Bugs Bunny and dozens of other characters. Each cartoon ended with the stuttering voice of Elmer Fudd saying, "Tha... Tha... That's all folks."

Those words were chiseled into his tombstone, but death does not end with a "that's all folks." Not only is there an eternity of consciousness awaiting every living person, there are eternal consequences, reverberations affecting the lives of countless individuals long after our own personal conclusion, our death.

RESERVATIONS IN WRITING

In the first sentences of this writing adventure, I expressed my personal reluctance in such an undertaking. First, who needs another book? My greatest concern has been the many repetitions of the personal pronouns I and me. But as this manuscript evolved, I became so self-conscious of the listings of the plethora of ailments God has so graciously allowed to pass across my threshold. My fear is that such an inventory would appear to be a solicitation for some pity or sympathy, or far worse, they would reveal subconscious, unrealized hypochondria.

Even in the converted man the truth remains that "the heart is desperately wicked, who can know it?" For any person to say, 'if I know my heart...' is foolhardy because, of a truth, no man really knows his heart. Every person has a daily battle with ego and as has been pointed out, that humility is that quality that when one thinks he has attained it, he just lost it. But my desire is that these ramblings are shared that He might be exalted and that it will emphasize that His grace is more than sufficient.

'TIS GRACE THUS FAR'

Before the first page of this manuscript was begun, I had determined that this would be the title of this autobiography, "Tis Grace...Thus Far." Four words from one verse of the great hymn, 'Tis grace hath brought me safe thus far, and grace will lead me home.' After all, what is grace? It is too simplistic and inadequate to limit grace to the old definition, "unmerited favor" thus giving the impression that it is only an attribute of our Holy God. It is that, but oh so much more than that. Grace is not just an attribute of God, but it is also the Divine activity, the supernatural activity of the Sovereign. When Paul groans for the removal of the hideous thorn from his flesh, and he prays for this for three long seasons and the answer comes from the Father saying, "My grace is sufficient."

It gives little comfort to limit grace to only mean unmerited favor until one understands the Father to be saying, "My Divine, supernatural, enablement is sufficient to handle this suffering and to glorify me in this weakness."

As has been pointed out, the Apostle Paul's thorn is never identified, lest a person limit this grace of God to only Paul's agony and consider his personal agony beyond the scope of this mentioned divine ability of our God. What comfort to realize that nothing that we will ever encounter or whatever befalls us will be beyond the adequacy of the Grace of God.

A SURPRISING CONFESSION

Mother, still lovely in retirement years.

Probably thirty years had passed since that night in November of 1953 when I opened the front door of my home and entered the dark hallway. It was after midnight and rather than try to sneak back to my bedroom without my mother calling me to her bedside and giving me the third degree as to my night's conduct, I rousted her from her bed with a message. "Mother, when I graduate in February, I am not leaving home, but I am going to college and preach." Mother, Carolyn and I, and her Mom were discussing that event, now some three decades later. For the very first time I heard my mother make a surprising confession. "And when you came home that night and told me how you had recommitted your life to the Lord and that you were going to preach, I lay awake all night and cried and said," "Lord, he will never make it."

Well, these fifty-eight years later I realize she was right on target. I haven't 'made it'. But ah, by the supernatural Grace of our living God, we have made it. That Grace that saved me and sought after me during those teenage years of rebellion, that Grace that forgave the Prodigal, put on a robe of righteousness, that Grace that gave me a grace gift of preaching offers me the ability to say, with weeping humility, we have made it. Do I mean, by that seemingly boastful statement, that I dare consider myself a success? Absolutely not! But, by that Divine, enabling Grace, He has permitted me to be faithful. He has opened doors of opportunity beyond my wildest imagination. Many, many people have confessed Jesus as Lord and Savior. Multitudes have recommitted their lives to Jesus and lest I ever fall victim of Satanic pride and consider myself successful, He brings to my simple mind how He alone is worthy of praise and recognition.

SAD LESSONS IN THE SCHOOL OF HUMILITY

I reflect upon a particular pastor with whom I served in revival a number of times. The fellowship of that church was one of genuine enthusiasm. Attendance was always exceptional. Before I stood to preach, there was a faith confidence that people would be converted, because his people were witnessing day by day. Not one time did I ever share the Word, morning or night, that there was not a consciousness of the presence of the blessed Holy Spirit.

I often thought to myself, and said to others, that if God ever led me to serve as pastor of a local church, I would want that church to be my desired pattern. In years to come it was discovered, and made public, that the pastor had had adulterous relationships with women in the church. He had even stooped to betrayal with wives of his own staff members. I rehearse this sorted tale to remind myself and others that if God can use the preaching of His Word to bring souls to Christ through a scoundrel like this, why should I strut, vainly considering myself other than a weak instrument that He has chosen to use. The Glory is altogether His and His alone!

I shudder as I recall the experience and testimony of an evangelist. Upon his release from a Florida prison he wrote a book detailing his conversion during his incarceration. In the autobiography, he vividly described how his Jewish parents in Boston had denounced him as their son and conducted his funeral because he had announced Jesus as Savior, Messiah and Lord. His charismatic dynamism opened the doors to some of the largest churches in America and he shared his testimony before tens of thousands at a Southern Baptist Convention. Later, it was discovered that he was again imprisoned in the Carolinas and upon investigation it was revealed he was not Jewish, was not from Boston, his messages were largely plagiarized and his life was a complete sham.

But the one single most important thing he did, he preached the Gospel, though through unsaved lips, and our God blessed His Word with the salvation of souls. No wonder, if God can speak through Balaam's ass, which happened to be a female and had an advantage, He can even speak though an unconverted preacher. Unusual? Yes, but such knowledge should clip the wings of any prideful preacher and cause him "to stand in amazement of Jesus the Nazarene, and wonder how He would or could use a sinner unclean." I have heard it said many times that God will not use a dirty vessel, but even at our very best we come so short of His glorious character. He shares His Glory with no man and woe to that individual who dares to think of himself or his abilities a necessity to God.

As I reflect on these nearly sixty years of ministry, I can recall the names of more than thirty men, individuals whom I have known personally, who started well, but fell by the wayside and sadly became what the Apostle Paul designates as 'castaways,' promising pastors and evangelists who have disqualified themselves from God called ministries. Most of them became victims of moral impurity, others captured by greed. I do not stand in harsh judgment of these individuals, because I am acutely aware that apart from the Grace of our God and Savior, my name would perhaps head the list.

For all of His Children, "It is only by Grace *thus far* and Grace (alone) will lead us home."

CHAPTER 39

INSTRUMENTS OF GOD

I dare not close this volume without expressing sublime appreciation for individuals whom our Lord has used to influence and shape my life and ministry.

Dr. Mabre Lunceford

Sadly, when I recommitted my life to Jesus and surrendered to His call to preach, I fell prey to an attitude of legalism. It was not a legalism of a works salvation, but rather an outlook of do's and don'ts, and I was the judge of what was right and wrong, not only for myself, but also for others. I did not harbor a self-righteousness, but I was not very tolerant of those who did not share my 'convictions.' In my enormous immaturity I interpreted, 'come ye out from among them,' as being like Jesus.

It was in my freshman year at Howard College that I sat under the tutelage of Dr. Mabre Lunceford, Professor of Bible. As he stood tall and erect, I was captured by his wisdom and kindness of spirit. Day-by-day, week-by-week and month-by-month I witnessed his demeanor, his revealing of the Person and character of the Savior. Often, I sought his counsel, guidance and companionship. Though he has now gone to be with his Lord, he is still remembered as one of the most, if not the most, Godly man I have ever encountered.

Dr. Lunceford conducted our wedding ceremony and when our third son was born, we chose the name Barry Lunceford Britt. You can imagine the humiliation he faced in years to come with that middle name. Buddies cruelly kidded him and often Barry asked, "Why did you stick me with that name

Lunceford?" Parents can be often so insensitive in naming their children. A number of years later, Barry yielded to God's call to preach and he too sat under the instruction of Mabre Lunceford. He apologized to Mabre for the resentment he held in his heart for that name and came home thanking us for the privilege of being Barry Lunceford Britt.

I thank God for a man who, with no pretense, a man without guile, revealed the person and character of the Lord Jesus Christ in a quiet and demonstrative way.

Clifford Matthews

A God called country boy from the city of Troy, deep in the southeast corner of the state of Alabama. His face had been scared and disfigured from a fire in the early days of his youth. But the ugliness of the scar was lost in the enthusiastic joy of Jesus, which radiated his face. We were drawn together like magnets and shared sweet fellowship in our mutual love for Jesus. I helped Cliff get a job with the National Shirt Shop in downtown Birmingham. During our lunch break he would drag me down to the corner of Second Avenue and Twentieth Street and hand gospel tracts to the crowds that passed by. It was a day in which such were well received and few tracts were simply tossed away. A few times, as small crowds would gather, we would boldly lift voices and preach in the midst of honking horns and the rush of the people. Surprisingly, a number of individuals would linger, captured by the Sprit, and ask us to pray with them to receive Jesus.

Clifford Matthews was the first individual to take the time and sit down with me and lead me down what is called The Roman Road, a simple method to lead an individual to the saving knowledge of salvation offered by Jesus. With few alterations to that plan of instructions, I can honestly say I have seen thousands of persons on trains, planes, and busses, and kids on bicycles, in homes, and places of businesses, men of great means and men of no means, bow their heads with tears and be swept into the Kingdom. Thank God for Clifford, for tutoring a young city boy on how to open the gates of glory, armed with no more than a New Testament and the anointing of Jesus to lead others into the Kingdom.

Charles Merry Christmas

An unusual name for an unusual man; somber, serious, not given to levity, but always revealing the joy of the Lord. We were so different in personality, yet drawn to one another by the love of Christ. He invited me for several revival meetings and more than once would kindly rebuke me for statements I would make, in what Dr. W. A. Criswell called 'the heat of inspiration.' Each admonishment was always appropriate and needed for a young and immature evangelist.

One day as we were knocking on doors, sharing the Good News of the Gospel, several small children in the neighborhood gathered around the Godly pastor to hold his hand and to hug him about the knees and express their love. As we walked away he made a statement that will forever ring in my ears. "I wish I was the man those children think I am." It is a testimony of the true humility that best characterized the genuineness of this noble man of God.

His zeal for souls, his passionate prayer life, his holy boldness, was just what this young preacher needed. Charles Merry Christmas, an unusual name for an unusual man, a man who challenged me to hunger for authentic humility.

Merle Packham

My life and ministry has given me opportunity to be in the company of many 'men of God', but not a multitude of Godly men. But no individual has impacted my personal life more than Brother Merle Packham. He had little formal education, but was a gentleman of great wisdom. His bookshelves contained few volumes, but in that limited collection were several well-worn Bibles. For more than twenty years he was the pastor of a small church in Central Florida. The building was a wooden structure with a rusting tin roof, located at the end of an unpaved sand road, in the middle of nowhere. I was privileged to be invited for two eight-day meetings to minister to that fellowship of believers. Recognizing his insight and perception, I sought every opportunity for his personal fellowship. Not once can I recall an answer given to my seeking soul that did not begin with, 'Brother Britt', and then would follow a flow of Scriptures that were imbedded in his head and heart. Although twenty years my senior, he always referred to me as Brother Britt. Diminutive in spirit, he epitomized a true Bible scholar, with a heart for the Savior.

George Vlahakes

Formally mentioned in this memoir, George was a ministerial student at old Howard College in eastern Birmingham. He rented a room in our home in the mid forties. Recently converted out of the Greek Orthodox Church, he was all but disowned by his family. Though his lifestyle was one of near poverty, he enjoyed the riches of Christ. He encouraged me in the Lord, gave me books by men such as Dwight L. Moody, R. A. Torrey, and other spiritual giants of a bygone era. He carried me with him to downtown rescue missions and wept as he preached to men of the street. I was only eleven years old, but at three score and ten plus, I will forever be grateful that God sent him into our home and the impact he had on my life. As a young boy, he was my only spiritual mentor and one of the few adult, positive role models so desperately needed for a kid who had sensed God's call to preach.

Don Shoff

A fellow seminary student and beloved friend, Don was a graduate of a fundamental, almost extreme, Bible college. Many of the alumnae of that institution exhibited a harsh, judgmental attitude but this dear brother in Christ has always manifested a kind spirit of Jesus, without compromising his strong biblical convictions. With no pretense, he is an articulate Christian gentleman who has given his latter years to mentoring fellow ministers of the Gospel. God has used him and his wife Judy to encourage me in my most needed moments. Many miles now separate us, but I look forward to sharing their sweet fellowship in our Lord's Heaven.

Brother Jess Hendley

As a sophomore at Howard College, I visited a revival meeting at Lakewood Baptist Church in eastern Birmingham. The evangelist was an anointed, bold man of God by the name of Dr. Jess Hendley. Never, had I ever heard such a brilliant prophet of the Lord speak with such authority and brokenhearted compassion. I was introduced to him by the pastor, and did not see nor hear from him for many years, but I never forgot that gravelly voice and the genuine compassion, so evident as he pleaded for the souls of men and women.

More than twenty years later I had the honor of inviting him to conduct two conferences on Bible prophecy at Hilldale Baptist Church. At the conclusion of the studies of the books of Revelation and Daniel more than thirty people were converted in each meeting. Brilliance beyond description, kindness with few equals and a zeal for the lost that was evident to all who heard him preach or were fortunate to share in his fellowship. Brother Jess was one of the few men who could open a Greek New Testament and share the wealth of the Scriptures, letting the language paint spectacular images upon the canvas of the listener's mind. Many hours I sat in his motel room and feasted on The Book and was blessed by his sweet fellowship. Few of his tribe remain with us today, but never has there existed an era when such prophets of God were needed.

Junior Hill

For the uninitiated, that is really his name, Junior. There was no senior, it was not a nickname. That is simply how he was tagged at birth. The name seemed most unlikely because most of his adult life he struggled with a battle of the bulge. He was not large, he was humongous. Lest you think I am being highly insensitive or cruel, one only needed to be in his presence or hear him preach, listen to him joke about his size, and then seize the moment to probe the hearts of the lost with a powerful presentation of the Gospel. I write as if my recollections of Junior are in the past tense, but that is only because God has given him the victory over his obesity and at this present time he weighs less than yours truly, much to my chagrin.

I place Junior in this sacred list because of his finest virtue. We met at Howard College, became and still are the best of friends. I conducted revival meetings in nearly every church he pastored. The first meeting was in a little church in North Alabama. For eight days I lodged in his mother's modest home and thus observed his character close up. Now, for more than forty years he has traveled this country from coast to coast, border to border, heralding the good news of Jesus. Doors have opened for him, literally around the world. God has allowed him to preach in many of the largest churches in America. He has shared the message of encouragement to tens of thousands at the Southern Baptist Convention meetings. On the average, he ministers three and four times a week as he criss-crosses our nation. And yet he goes to some of the smallest churches several times a year.

Now past three score and ten, dealing with the consequences of the toil of so many years on the road, he is still the same Junior Hill I met at Howard College fifty-five years ago. Many preachers can endure the common life experiences or even failure and keep on plugging, maintaining a spirit of humility, but rare indeed is that man of God who can stand before the multitudes, receiving the applause and accolades of so called success, and maintain genuine humility. That is Brother Junior's finest virtue, a man poor in spirit, but walking in the wealth of family and friends, entrusted with the gift of an evangelist, a weapon being faithfully wielded to the present day. He is my hero.

Daryl Jones

Three decades have now passed since my very best friend went to be with his Lord. As a veteran of WWII, Daryl was saved when he was past thirty years of age and very shortly after that was called of God to preach. He owned a grocery and feed store in Leeds, Alabama and from all reports was a man's man, fouled mouthed, hard drinking, always ready for a fight, yet a man respected as a person of integrity and a mind that was brilliant.

I met Daryl during my freshman year in college. Though a dozen years older than me, we became close friends. Tragically, his wife had died in a freak automobile wreck just weeks after his call to preach. He became the single father to his lovely daughter and two boys, a difficult and challenging task. In months to come he married a young, multi-talented lady in the church. Because of their difference in age, the wagging tongues and rumor mills made it necessary for him to resign his church and become pastor of another local church.

It has been said that birds of a feather flock together and we two birds shared a joy and addiction for bass fishing. On most Saturdays, from just before sun up until the setting of the old orange ball, we were pounding the banks of Lay Lake on the Coosa River. Jones was a bass expert and whetted my appetite for the scaly creation more than ever. Through the coming years, we spent literally thousands of hours chunking our baits toward bassy looking abodes and most often with great result.

We labored through Southwestern Seminary together and shared many happy hours with our families joined in sweet fellowship. For years he and Eudora and Carolyn and I attended Evangelism Conferences, Southern Baptist Conventions, State Conventions, and vacationed together.

The impressions and the impact upon my life go far beyond the experiences of racing down a waterway. No, that which prepared my life for ministry the most was his diligence in what is called *expository preaching.* That is simply and pronouncedly taking each book of the Bible, and carefully and with integrity *exposing* its truth verse-by-verse and chapter-by-chapter. Many pastors have a thought come to mind or an issue arises that they feel needs addressing, and that minister simply searches to find a text to support his preconceived idea. Add a few illustrations, insert some humor and many individuals will leave the sanctuary satisfied, but spiritually starving to death, and that with little awareness of their spiritual poverty.

Topical sermons have their place at times, but it is the consistent book-by-book, verse-by-verse preaching that wins the lost, grows the saints and best glorifies the Lord Jesus to the Glory of the Father. This style of proclamation demands countless hours of solitude and study. Too many ministers find this too demanding or sadly, they pastor a people too selfish to provide the time for such preparation.

Sunday morning, Sunday night and Wednesday night, this man of God never failed to stand behind the sacred desk and boldly speak, "Thus saith the Lord", and speak that with great conviction. If there was any deserved compliment as to my attempt in preaching, it can be traced to Daryl Jones and the instruction he consciously and unconsciously contributed to me by the Grace of God.

"AND OTHERS"

Twice, in the eleventh chapter of Hebrews, the writer uses that phrase, "and others," as he heralds the faith of the heroes and there are many others that God brought into my pathway to impact my life and ministry. But again, as the writer said, "And what shall I say more, for the time would fail me to tell," of those that to whom I am indebted for all eternity.

First and foremost among those 'others', I am indebted to my Mom, Geraldine (Jerry) Britt. It is with shame and regret that I recall the days when, in my rebellion, I brought grief and sadness to the best friend a boy or man will ever have. For some years, she was not the most spiritual individual, but she related how that during my seminary years, God made some real differences in her life. Her Lord and her church became very precious to her. She became a warrior of prayer for her 'preacher boy.' Too late, I really came to appreciate the sacrifices she made for my brother and me. As related earlier, she went to work to support the family almost immediately after she became a widow. She labored until she was seventy years old and then retired from her position with the Social Security Department. During all those years, she never missed a night in preparing supper for the family. Although she left home early in the morning and worked eight or more hours, I cannot remember a time when a hot meal was not on the table. Thank the Lord for those hissing pressure cookers and canned biscuits. Not one time can I recall her complaining or griping about the difficulty of her tasks or the lonely hours she endured while I was away in Seminary and my brother away in the Air Force and then jobs that took him all over the U.S.A.

She enjoyed her retirement years and relished taking trips with her friends, mainly those with whom she had labored. In later years she began to deal with health issues, the complication of heart problems and a number of strokes. She finally agreed to allow a live-in caregiver, but fiercely fought for her independence. After a debilitating stroke, she insisted on being moved to a nursing home. She put up a good front, but we knew she was not happy. Needing the care that only such an institution could provide, she lived for less than two weeks in that facility. When I received an emergency call on a Sunday night I drove with haste and rushed into her room. She was still sitting up in her bed with a slight smile radiating her face, and I realized she had slipped into the arms of Jesus only moments before. Sitting beside her, I tried to express my sincere appreciation and gratefulness for her service and sacrifice far beyond the call of duty. Only Jesus will love you with unconditional love like a mother.

THE OLD PROSPECTOR

In my fondest dream, I could have never imagined the delightsome adventure of His plan for my life. From before that evening in 1953 when He graciously drew this Prodigal back into the fold, and especially since that blessed November night, I have felt like an old gold prospector that ventured into an aged mineshaft and discovered a seam of the precious ore. Every step into the passageway reveals a wider and ever enlarging and expanding layer of the valuable find. The only regrets of the journey have been those times of disobedience or indifference. With bowed head and hopefully a heart of humility, I say, "Thank you, Lord Jesus!"

The End